CW00457119

CHALDON HERRING

Writers in a Dorset Landscape

JUDITH STINTON

BLACK DOG BOOKS

© Judith Stinton 1988 & 2004

First published 1988 by The Boydell Press
New edition 2004 published by Black Dog Books

ISBN 09528839 8 8

British Library Cataloguing in Publication Data

Stinton, Judith,
Chaldon Herring: Writers in a Dorset Landscape.
1. Literary landmarks — England —Chaldon Herring (Dorset)
I. Title
942.3'36 PRIIO.C/

The Powys Society exists to promote the study and appreciation of the Powys
family. For further details write to the Secretary, Peter J. Foss, 82 Linden Road,
Gloucester, GL1 5HD.

The Sylvia Townsend Warner Society exists to promote the study and appreciation
of Sylvia Townsend Warner. For further details write to the Secretary,
Eileen Johnson, 2 Vicarage Road, Dorchester, Dorset, DT1 1LH.

Printed and bound in Great Britain by
Biddles Ltd., *www.biddles.co.uk*.

For
Gill King
with love and thanks

'It was an extraordinary place: extraordinary things happened there and extraordinary people were to be found there; and to everyone according to his capacity it gave according to his need.'

Valentine Ackland, *For Sylvia*

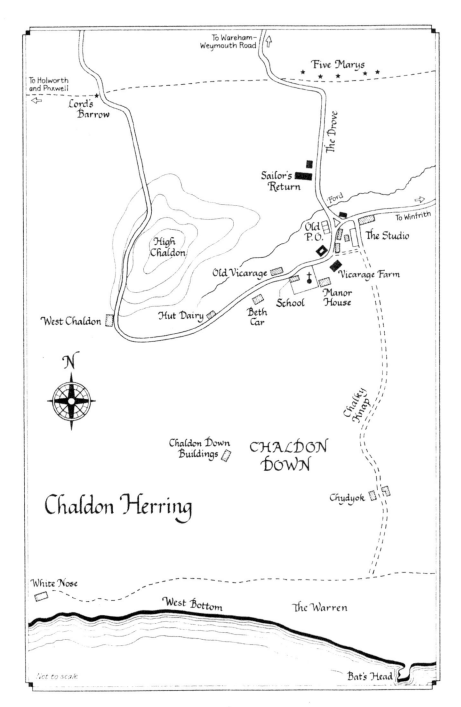

To Wareham–
Weymouth Road

Five Marys

To Holworth
and Poxwell

Lord's
Barrow

The Drove

Sailor's
Return

Ford

To Winfrith

Old
P.O.

The Studio

High
Chaldon

Old Vicarage

Vicarage Farm

School

Manor
House

West Chaldon

Hut Dairy

Beth
Car

N

Chalky Knap

Chaldon Down
Buildings

CHALDON
DOWN

Chaldon Herring

Chydyok

White Nose

West Bottom

The Warren

Not to scale

Bat's Head

Contents

Acknowledgements

Many people have helped in the shaping of this book. In particular I would like to acknowledge the assistance of:

Mr E. E. Bissell, Mr K. R. Bakes, David Brown, Louise de Bruin, Gerard Casey, the staff of Dorset County Library and Dorset Record Office, Paul Ensom and Roger Peers of Dorset County Museum, Oliver Garnett, Peter Powys Grey, David Grylls, Kenneth Hopkins, Peter Kemp, Gill King, Julian King, the staff of Senate House Library, University of London, Janet Machen, Rosemary Manning, David Muir, the late Mrs Lucy Penny, Francis and Sally Powys, and the staff of the Harry Ransom Humanities Research Centre, University of Texas at Austin.

Special thanks should go to my sister Ros Stinton for preparing the index, to Garold Sharpe for his generous contribution to the work in progress, and to the villagers of Chaldon, especially Ken and Josie Blandamer, Mr J. Cobb, the late Mrs Florence Legg, Mrs Hytie Mackintosh, the late Mrs Peggy Marx, Rowland and Betty Miller, and Jim Pitman.

Above all, I'd like to thank Philip Lord, who, despite hearing about little else for two years, has never failed to show a lively interest, and Kevin Crossley-Holland my editor at Boydell, for his sustained, tactful and imaginative support.

Judith Stinton
London, 1988

Second Edition
The author would again like to acknowledge all those who contributed to the first edition. Some of them have also helped with the second edition, as have David Ashford, Griffin Beale, Judith Bond, Glen Cavaliero, Richard Garnett, Jean Harvey, Kate Hebditch, Morine Krissdottir, the Marx Memorial Library, Sheila Milton, Richard de Peyer, Susanna Pinney, John Powys, Theodore Scutt and Anthony Ward. Finally I would especially like to thank my publisher Peter Tolhurst for his careful and imaginative preparation of this new edition.

The author and publisher would like to thank the following for permission to reproduce copyright material: The Whittington Press for Gwenda Morgan's front cover & p 101 wood-engraving; the Harry Ransom Humanities Research Center, University of Texas at Austin (as owners only); John Powys and Theodore Scutt for the Estate of T.F.Powys and Chatto & Windus Ltd; John Powys for the Estate of John Cowper Powys and Village Press. To the Estate of the authors and to Chatto & Windus for excerpts from *For Sylvia*, and *The Nature of the Moment* by Valentine Ackland, from *The Salutation, Whether a Dove or Seagull, Lolly Willowes, Diaries* and *Letters* by Sylvia Townsend Warner, and from *Mr Tasker's Gods, Mark Only, Unclay, Mr Weston's Good Wine, Innocent Birds, Kindness in a Corner* and *Mockery Gap* by Theodore Powys. To Susanna Pinney, copyright holder, the Estate of Sylvia Townsend Warner. To Sally Connely and to the Society of Authors as literary representatives of the Estate of Llewelyn Powys for quotations from his work. To John Powys for the Estate of Philippa (Katie) Powys. To A.P. Watt Ltd on behalf of the executors of the Estate of David Garnett for quotations from *The Familiar Faces* and *The Sailor's Return*. To Jonathan Cape on behalf of the Estate of Gerald Brenan for quotations from *Personal Record*. To the executors of the Estate of Gamel Woolsey. To John Powys as literary representative of the Estate of Alyse Gregory for permission to quote from the unpublished journals and from the letters from Valentine Ackland. To Peter Owen, London, and to Belinda Humfrey (ed.) for an extract from *Recollections of the Powys Brothers*. To Belinda Humfrey and to the *Powys Review*, that invaluable source for any student of the Powys family, for excerpts from 'Theodore Powys and Some Friends at East Chaldon' and 'East Chaldon and T. F. Powys' by Sylvia Townsend Warner, and from 'Conversations with Theodore' by Llewelyn Powys. To the *Powys Review* and Theodora Scutt for quotations from 'Theodore Powys, 1934 - 1953'.

Every attempt has been made to trace copyright holders, and any omission is unintentional.

Illustrations
The author is most grateful to the following for supplying illustrations:
David Brown, no 50; Gerard Casey, no 31; Common Ground, nos 79 & 80; Michael Copmpton, no 25; Dorset County Museum, nos 6, 10, 22, 23, 36, 37, 45, 49, 64, & 65; and Powys Society Collection, nos 4, 35, 42, 52, 53, 68, 69, 71, 75 & 76; and Susanna Pinney, copyright holder, nos 56, & 59; Fitzwilliam Museum, no 3; Oliver Garnett, no 18; Richard Garnett, nos 13, 16, 17, 19, 26, 27, 28 & 72; Wyndham Goodden, nos 30, 54 & 66; Morine Krissdottir, nos 43, 46 & 47; Philip Lord, nos 12 & 73; Rosemary Manning, nos 58 & 74; National Portrait Gallery, no 57; Janet Machen Pollock, nos 32 & 60; John Powys, no 24; Judith Stinton, no 14; Peter Tolhurst, nos 7, 9, 29, 33, 34, 40, 41, 44, 55, 62, 67, 70 & 78; University of Texas, nos 15 & 51; University of London Library, no 8.

Chaldon Herring

The Green Valley

Here in the green scooped valley I walk to and fro.
In all my journeyings I have not seen
A place so tranquil, so green;
And yet I think I have seen it long ago,
The grassy slopes, and the cart-track winding, so.

O now I remember it well, now all is plain,
Why twitched my memory like a dowser's rod
At waters hidden under sod.
When I was a child they told me of Charlemagne,
Of Gan the traitor, and Roland outmarched and slain.

Weeping for Roland then, I scooped in my spirit
A scant green Roncesvalles, a holy ground,
Which here in Dorset I've found;
But finding, I knew it not. The years disinherit
Their children. The horn is blown, but I do not hear it.

Sylvia Townsend Warner

Introduction

In 1901 Theodore Powys gave up his Suffolk farm and went to live at
Studland in Dorset. He was not to stay there long. Three years later he was
on the move again.

... when even that picturesque place became overrun with summer tourists, he took his
stick from his chimney-corner and set out to find some unpretentious village, where he
would be altogether free from molestation. He walked on and on, over the downs. He
went into Corfe, into Kimmeridge, into Arishmell Bay, until eventually he arrived at
Winfrith, and from there debouched to East Chaldon, which very possibly is the most
hidden village in Dorset.

Llewelyn Powys, Skin for Skin

East Chaldon, *alias Chaldon Herring* (as the old books would have
it), is still today an out-of-the-way place, blocked from the main road by
its bony shoulder of down, with a lane, once seven-gated, looping
round. For a while, though, the arrival of Theodore Powys was to bring
East Chaldon more visitors than it had ever received before, many of
them making the village their home, if only for a few, impressionable
weeks. Bohemian Bloomsbury and elegant London society swept down
upon it, generating in their movements more letters, diaries, articles
and, above all, fiction about the place than a thousand years of history
had produced.

Probably because of its remote position, Chaldon Herring has in fact
no history of any national significance. Most of its people lived and
died unrecorded, except for those who owned or sold the village lands.
The Herring of Chaldon's name comes not because of its proximity to
the unseen, fish-filled sea, but through the Normandy family of Harang
or Haryng (their French parish was called 'La Ferrière Harenc') who

were early landlords of the village, and who gave their name as well to Winterborne Herringston, Langton Herring and Herrison in Charminster, all of which they sometime owned. The arms of the family, 'viz. Three herrings haurient in fess' (erect with upright heads) can still be seen, hanging out of their element, on the fifteenth century font at Winterborne Whitechurch.

1. Harang coat of arms.

2. Weld coat of arms.

The holder of 'Calvedon' (one of the many variants of the name) at Domesday was King William. Shortly afterwards it passed into the hands of the Herrings. The first member of the family to be named in the records was Terricus Harang, who around 1172 gave 3 $^1/_2$ virgates of land in Chaldon to help found Bindon Abbey: over the years the family made several other gifts. One highly unsavoury Herring was Terricus's son, Philip, who in the reign of King John was convicted of the murder of 'a certain William, the clerk'. He was outlawed for his crime, but pardoned later.

Chaldon was in the liberty (or group of manors) of Bindon Abbey, which owned land there other than that given by the Herrings. The ancient settlement of Grange Farm belonged to Bindon until the abbey's suppression in 1539. Standing alone now, Grange Farm was once part of East Chaldon village and had a chapel, by 1801 incorporated into a house and now demolished.

In the same liberty was the separate manor of West Chaldon or Chaldon Boys (named after the family of De Bosco or Boys who held West Chaldon following the Conquest). West Chaldon, now no more than a farm and its cottages, was once too a separate parish, united in 1446 with Chaldon Herring for the reason that 'the issues of Chaldon Boys' had been declared 'insufficient to sustain a rector'. After this, the rector of the second, larger parish was expected 'weekly, and on the feast of St. Nicholas, to whom this church was dedicated, [to] celebrate mass in the chancel here, and repair it.. ' That was the beginning of a swift decline for West Chaldon church. By 1460 only the chancel remained and there were no further burials after 1466. During nineteenth and twentieth century rebuilding and alterations at the farm, quantities of human bones were discovered to its west, seeming to indicate the northerly site of the long-vanished church. (There are also remains of other medieval settlement.)

The last of the Herrings, John, died in 1455, by which time the family's possessions in the village were centred on East Chaldon Farm. John's daughter, Elizabeth, married Henry Russell, and their family became the heirs. By 1610 the village still belonged to the Russells, passing on through the hands of the Marquis of Worcester, 'Charles Price, gent.' and the Duke of Beaufort. In 1728 Richard Gostelowe rebuilt the manor house (or Grange) which for many years was in use as a farm. It was one of the items sold by the Duke of Beaufort in 1789 to Thomas Weld, whose family still own much of Chaldon Herring.

Farming has always been its way of life, though traces of other activities linger. Unlike some larger villages in the nineteenth century, Chaldon was never well-endowed with shops, generally possessing no more than one or two. The population, which averaged around 300 throughout this period, was just big enough to support a blacksmith. Three men named Edward Sturmey, father, son and grandson, ran the smithy, a single-storey building on the corner of the green. There was another smithy at West Chaldon, of brick and tile, but that has now disappeared.

Around the village, clusters of chalkpits and old lime-kilns pockmark the hillside, while on the cliffs the Warren and Newlands Warren keep their names and some of their inhabitants. They mark the efforts by 'Calcraft, Esq.' around 1815 to create a breeding-ground for rabbits, much to the fury of the local farmers. The rabbits were supposed to be kept out of the cornfields by 'low banks with a hedge on the top'. These proved an inadequate barrier - and an all-too-efficient breeding-ground for the animals. The farmers soon took matters into their own hands, assuming any rabbits they caught there to be their property, in an attempt 'to diminish their numbers as much as possible'. The farm labourers regarded the burrows more favourably as a source of food - close by can be seen the remains of a trapper's dwelling known as 'Warren House' where many a rabbit met its end. (Pleasingly, a nineteenth century view of these cliffs has recently come to light - Samuel Palmer's oil painting 'On Chaldon Down', c 1840, probably completed after one of several sketching expeditions the artist made to the West Country around this time.)

More unlikely than rabbits, even in an age of prolific railway expansion, was the scheme of 1896 to build a light railway from Lulworth to Osmington. The route proposed was to navigate a series of difficult, beautiful and crumbling hills from West Lulworth, across the Warren, behind the White Nose coastguard station and Holworth House to a terminus at Osmington. The company also sought a working agreement with the South-Western Railway, their aim being a link with the larger company at Wolgret Junction, and running powers as far as Wareham. The scheme predictably came to nothing; the Warren was left to the rabbits and Chaldon to its inaccessibility.

3. *On Chaldon Down*, by Samuel Palmer, c.1840, oil on canvas, Fitzwilliam Museum, Cambridge.

4. Chaldon Landscape, wood engraving by C. C. Webb, c.1940.

Nowhere in England, though, as Theodore Powys was to discover, is ever safe from visitors. Perhaps he should have been warned by the events of 1830, when the village received its most exalted day-tripper of all time - a bored and boisterous Bourbon princess.

Chaldon Herring

The Clasped Skeletons

O why did we uncover to view
  So closely clasped a pair?
Your chalky bedclothes over you,
  This long time here!
       . . . . .

So long, beyond chronology,
  Lovers in death as 'twere,
So long in placid dignity
  Have you lain here!

Yet what is length of time? But dream!
  Once breathed this atmosphere
Those fossils near you, met the gleam
  Of day as you did here;

But so far earlier theirs beside
  Your life-span and career,
That they might style of yestertide
  Your coming here!

Thomas Hardy

CHAPTER ONE

The Five Marys

Chaldon is an old settlement; almost as old perhaps as the hills that gather round it, their green slopes hummocked with remains of an early occupation. The soil is thin, the past lies close to the surface and can be easily disturbed.

Not far beneath turf and feathered barley the knuckle of chalk is clenched. The earth-layer between them is flecked with flints, often worked into tools or weapons. They chequer the land in loosely-changing patterns, themselves incapable of change. Up on the cliffs, where the grassy mosaic of Celtic fields spills over into the sea, the flint-filled bottoms mark the site of ancient quarries. The flints are scattered everywhere, twenty thousand years old and ineradicable as the rabbits - or as weeds.

When compared to these stony, impermeable relics, the Five Marys, a group of barrows dating from the Late Bronze Age (1620-700 B.C.), seem rather recent. They are, though, the most conspicuous of all the prehistoric remains in Chaldon. Approach them, and they rise up mutely one by one - as if in dumbshow - signalling the northern limit of the village.

The Five Marys they are called, but the name is deceptive. There are, unmagically, at least six barrows in the group, while the word 'Marys' derives from the Anglo-Saxon *gemaere* or boundary mark. They are marked as the Five Meers on J. Taylor's *Map of Dorset*, 1765, and are spread in a straightish line along the former boundary which separated the parish of Chaldon from that of West Fossil.

Near to the barrows is a hawthorn tree, which was for the writer Llewelyn Powys a milestone in his walks.

It was dark before we reached the quarry, but, as we came over the Five Marys, at the point of the road where the old thorn bush is which has been bent like a well-used besom by a thousand gales from the south-west, the moon suddenly swung into view, like an enormous lantern, on the left of Flower's Barrow.

5. 'Folly Down' from the Five Marys. Frontispiece by George Charlton to T.F.Powys's *Mr Weston's Good Wine*, 1927.

Not many species of tree could survive the salt winds. A hedge of thorn, quickened by ash and holly, grows stubbornly along the boundary bank for much of its route. Close beside it there is a track, pre-Roman, which led from Poxwell Corner via the Five Marys to Winfrith and beyond. This road was a branch of the Southern Ridgeway and was in use until the early part of the twentieth century, one of a mesh of roads which covered the chalk cliffs and downs. Mostly deserted now, they have an air of ghostly activity. The Five Marys' road runs along a narrow ridge, not high, but on a platform above the surrounding fields.

Clear below, on Chaldon Meadow, can be seen the ribbed remains of the medieval village of Holworth. In winter, the sun's slanting rays reveal it most nakedly: the sunken outline of a street and the square sites of the houses, covering 13 acres altogether. A village called Holworth was a lively community in 1086, when the Domesday Book recorded its four cows and 224 sheep (Chaldon itself had 500 sheep). In 1958, when the village was excavated, it was discovered that the site was 'a maze of ditches' which had been constantly recut and dredged during the last years of life there in the 14th to 15th centuries, and the marshy nature of the site could well have been one reason for its abandonment. Although the story persists that Ringstead, the next deserted village along the chalk, was destroyed by French pirates in the Middle Ages, the most likely cause of both villages' depopulation was the Black Death. The Plague entered England at the nearby port of Melcombe Regis, Weymouth, in 1348 and severely afflicted the whole Dorset coast. During 1348-9, West Chaldon (still then a separate parish) lost its priest in December and again in May because of the pestilence.

6. The old ridgeway track beside the Five Marys.

A track cuts diagonally across the Holworth site to meet the road from the Five Marys which ends by Poxwell stone circle. This circle is a miniature one, only 14' in diameter, and set on the top of an oval-shaped barrow. Of the stones, which are probably all in place, only three are of any size. The rest are tiny and, it would seem, could be easily overlooked. Yet small as they are, huge claims have been made for them. In the nineteenth century, local antiquarians like William Barnes and Charles Warne remained undaunted by the circle's modest dimensions. It was, they claimed, a 'sepulchral memorial' or (more grandly) a place of sacrifice: 'a Druid's temple'. This was the most

9

popular explanation of the circle, and one which was wholeheartedly endorsed by Llewelyn Powys. He described the group of stones at Poxwell (or Puck's Well) as 'that stone circle put into place by other priests, centuries before any such extraordinary notion had come into God's head as to send down to earth His only-begotten son to be sacrificed by Himself, to Himself'. Powys often walked there with his brother Theodore, an outlandish travelling-companion.

One day Theodore commented upon the grass of his chosen habitation. 'I like this long, white, downland grass,' he said. 'Nothing ever eats it, and it's like the curious grey hairs of some old woman. It never gets wet. In summer I often roll in it.'

Llewelyn felt that the circle was best seen alone and at midnight. 'At such an hour each tree in the ancient Trenchard wood below stands clear under the stars, and it is as though the patient timber with its trembling leaves gave strength and understanding to the mind'. An even stranger experience was seeing the circle with his brother one hoary New Year's Eve.

Theodore entered the ring first, the shadow of his bowed figure - he had taken his old cloak about him - appearing, as it fell across the deep-sunken stones, like the shadow of some Biblical prophet, like the shadow of the prophet, Amos! And with what curious, prophetic eyes he squinnied up at the sky during those still, frosty moments!

This seer-ridden circle is the finish for the old road. It has made a memorable journey. The four-mile length of track is barnacled with tumuli (including the much-mutilated Lord's Barrow, which still marks a boundary of Chaldon Parish). Not just this track in fact, but the entire reach of the Southern Ridgeway could be mapped out by its earthworks alone. The Five Marys, like many another group, stands out so roundly because it is built on that narrow stretch of spine three hundred yards from the highest point of the hill. The effect of this is to silhouette the barrows against the skyline, so that they can be seen from the valley below, where their builders were probably to be found. Beneath glittering mounds the dead lay at peace, keeping faithful watch over the living.

Yet there must have been times in the last two centuries when the dead were very unquiet indeed. Their rest was more than likely to be disturbed: the barrow diggers were advancing.

Amongst the most chronicled of the diggers from the eighteenth century was William Stukeley, begetter of many a theory about the Druids, who had undertaken much of his early and valuable work in Dorset and Wiltshire (notably around Stonehenge). Stukeley was a pioneer, and in the Romantic

Age he was to have many, fervent successors, notably in the counties he himself had studied.

The sublime cliffs, the bleakly brooding downland, of remote and undiscovered Dorset called for exploration - and excavation. The conspicuous graves which starred the Ridgeway and the surrounding chalk would have been doubly enticing. The diggers might hope for all manner of treasure, plus the thrill of uncovering the skeletal remains of the unknown, unsung dead.

7. Poxwell stone circle.

Despite the rush, the serious study of archaeology was managing to make some progress. Sir Richard Colt Hoare, for instance, in his *Ancient Wiltshire* published between 1810-1821, was able to distinguish some of the various types of barrow (bowl, bell, saucer, pond) and also to identify the different levels of primary and secondary interment. But this was equally the age of the dilettante, when the vogue for antiquity-hunting (by genteel persons in search of an afternoon's entertainment) was at its height. Such people were not satisfied until they had acquired their share of fashionably bony curios. The dramatic scenery of the coast around Lulworth Cove was a favourite spot for this pastime. In 1790 the Reverend John Milner, 'assisted by Mr. Weld and other gentlemen' made short work of seventeen barrows near the Cove. Two of these, Rev. Milner noted, were found to be in a 'confused state' (he gives no details of how he left them). Another, on Hambury Tout, contained an unusually tall skeleton, about 6'6" in height which, in the stretched imaginings of his local diggers, grew to be seven or eight feet long.

There were further fanciful reports in 1833 when a number of barrows were opened at Monkton Farm, by Maiden Castle. Whilst delving into the stomach of one of his specimens, the archaeologist (an unsuccessful actor-dramatist named John Fitzgerald Pennie) declared that he had discovered some 'small kidney-shaped seeds' in an undigested state. When handed over to Dr. Lindley, curator of the Horticultural Society's gardens at Kew, they proved to be raspberry, and provided 'much fine fruit'.

With all this fruitful destruction of local earthworks which had lain mostly undisturbed, except by the plough, for centuries, it was hardly surprising that the Five Marys did not escape exploration. The archaeologist is more remarkable. Charles Warne gives his own account in *Celtic Tumuli of Dorset*, 1866.

On a branch of the Ridgeway, that supervenes between the village of East Chaldon and the hamlet of Forsel, is a group of tumuli, known locally as the Five Sisters or Marys.

Of these, two were examined under the direction of the Duchess of Berri and others attached to the suite of Charles X., who, driven from the throne of France, were then (as refugees) enjoying asylum in the spacious castle of Lulworth, which had been so liberally proferred them by Mr. Weld.

The owner of Lulworth Castle, and of the surrounding lands including (from 1789) most of Chaldon Herring, was Thomas Weld. He was also a Catholic - and a Cardinal in Rome, one of only two Englishmen to be so honoured since 1694. In his absence the estate was managed by his brother, Joseph. The Welds had been a staunch Catholic family for centuries. Cardinal Weld's father, another Thomas, had received special permission from George III (who visited Lulworth from his Weymouth residence) to build a chapel in the castle grounds. The King stipulated only that the chapel should not look like one, and what Fanny Burney called a 'Pantheon in miniature' still graces the park. Inside are galleries on Tuscan columns and a vast, celestial central dome. It is an elegant and dignified statement of faith.

Royal favours apart, the Welds did not escape persecution for this faith, both in minor and more sinister ways. Fining Catholics was an easy way of raising revenue for the state. Nor were they allowed to keep horses of a greater value than £5 (the Framptons of Moreton were for a time the nominal owners of the Lulworth stable). As Papists, the Welds were constantly under suspicion. In 1745 an attempt was made to implicate Edward Weld in the Jacobite Rebellion when a treasonable letter said to be written by him was recovered at Poole, and he was taken to London to be examined. 'An immediate and honourable discharge was a convincing proof of his innocence', Hutchins's *History of Dorset* triumphantly concludes. In 1803 a 'malicious and absurd' rumour that the Welds were harbouring Napoleon's brother, Jerome (who was in fact in America), ran through the neighbourhood. Like their guest, Charles X, the Welds had known fear of the mob.

Perhaps because of such incidents, the Weld family had a tradition of welcoming French Catholic refugees. Thomas Weld the elder gave Stonyhurst to exiled Jesuits from Liège. He likewise offered the house now known as Monastery Farm on the cliffs below Flower's Barrow to a group of French Trappist monks, who settled there for twenty-one years.

And now Thomas's son was welcoming the former King of France and his enormous suite. And not last among this royal horde, at least in her own odd eyes, was Marie-Caroline Louise Ferdinande, daughter of the sometime king of Naples and the Two Sicilies, and widow of the Duc de Berri.

The Duchesse de Berri had been widowed for ten long years, a highly dramatic decade both for herself and for France. Charles X, who succeeded in 1824, was a pious and pig-headed king whose reign brought fresh turbulence to France and stately dullness to the French court. The position of the Duchesse in this court, endangered as it was from time to time by her penchant for theatrical gestures, had been secured by the birth of a posthumous son, *l'enfant du miracle*, the so-called Henry V, adored grandson of Charles and the Bourbon heir. (He remained pretender to the French throne, a forlorn and exiled figure, until his death in 1883.) Naturally, his claims were enthusiastically upheld by his mother.

The young Duchesse de Berri found life in mourning at the French court somewhat restrictive. She was not pretty exactly, but possessed, it was said, *quelque chose de séduisant et d'entraînant*. Masses of fair hair, a white skin and 'the tiniest feet imaginable' added to this effect. Her main flaw (as witnessed by Madame de Boigne in her royal memoirs) was that one eye was smaller than the other. (Or, as the courtly Prince de Poix more gallantly expressed it, 'Possibly the left eye of the Duchesse de Berri is a little larger than the right'.)

For many, her charm lay in her youthful vivacity and spontaneity. Brought up in the tiny Neapolitan court amidst peasants and beggars, she had a horror of the pretentiously formal which must sometimes have made silk-and-satin Parisian life intolerable. Such an upbringing, though, left her unsophisticated and extravagant. Madame de Boigne - not, it must be confessed, the most

8. Marie-Caroline, Duchesse de Berri.

devoted of her admirers - described the Duchesse as a 'giggly schoolgirl' who had arrived in her eagerly-adopted country 'in a state of complete and total ignorance'. The education she received in France left her barely literate. Nor, regrets de Boigne, was Marie-Caroline taught her duties as a princess: her older, unfaithful husband merely spoilt her.

Yet the Duchesse could read well enough to enjoy the novels of Sir Walter Scott and to be affected by them. She saw herself as a heroine; indeed she did not lack the courage to be one. Once when she was out driving with the Duc and their horses unexpectedly bolted, the Duchesse, much to her husband's amazement, showed no fear at all. Again, in 1820, on hearing the news that her husband had been stabbed, she rushed immediately to the aid of the dying man, heedless of blood and danger. 'The boarding-school girl of the morning', wrote Madame de Boigne, 'became suddenly heroic'.

One of the most disconcerting aspects of this heroic stance was the Duchesse's predilection for appearing *sans chemise*. She delighted in male costume, in which she would go out shooting rabbits. She also appeared at Trianon before the troops (who could usually be relied on to admire her) in men's attire, with two pistols in her belt and one in her hand. This appearance was afterwards repeated *avec fracas* - and to distinctly less effect - before Charles X. The King had more serious matters on his mind. During the July Revolution of 1830, he kept stubbornly to his rooms at Saint-Cloud, oblivious of the angry crowds which had gathered in the city, hurling pianos and commodes from their windows at the troops below. Quite undaunted, the Duchesse had to be dissuaded from showing herself to the people. She never for a moment doubted the success of her own charms. Another love of Marie-Caroline's was for masked balls, and at her most celebrated and prophetic one in 1829 she made her entrance as that queen of tragedy, Mary Stuart. In the following year, strangely enough, she was herself to taste exile with the rest of the court at Holyrood.

But first of all she went to Lulworth. The castle, though late Tudor fantasy rather than Scottish baronial, must have pleased the Duchesse. (Not so Charles, who is supposed to have said ungraciously on seeing his place of shelter, '*Voilà, la Bastille!*')

Great crowds awaited the French King and his entourage when they reached Poole Harbour on August 22, en route for the castle. Charles had to be encouraged to disembark, the captain explaining that the ship was too big to enter the crab-shaped cove at Lulworth. Thus forced to land, Charles scuttled straight to his place of shelter (where two hundred more people were lined up to view him). Meanwhile the Duchesse was spending the night at the London Tavern in Poole. On leaving the next day she expressed her thanks to the Poole crowd. 'Their conduct', reported the *Dorset County Chronicle*, 'should never be effaced from her memory'. Then off she swept to Lulworth.

Joseph Weld may soon have regretted his own generosity. There were so many in the French court. The overflow from the castle had to be billeted at Heffleton (now Hethfelton) House and possibly on Brownsea Island as well. There was also the question of how long they intended to stay. 'It would seem from their movements and arrangements that they anticipate a residence of some little duration' the *Chronicle* remarked.

9. Lulworth Castle from the south.

For their part, the French visitors were soon to discover the drawbacks of the 'spacious accommodation' so praised by Charles Warne. Madame de Gontaut, tutor to the young Duc and his sister, put a noble face on the situation. They had found the castle to be in ruins, but fortunately, 'as the weather was fine we could sleep there, and even in a storm we could put up umbrellas'.

Fear of the rabble (and of bailiffs) meant that the King rarely left the park, where he would sometimes do a little shooting. The rest of the party made a thorough exploration of the surrounding area. They were, as Mary Frampton noted, 'great walkers'. (She was surprised by the shabbiness of their appearance. When the Duchesse d'Angoulême called on the family at Moreton, the Framptons' butler mistook her for a lady's maid - though on closer inspection the daughter of Louis XVI was unmistakeable. She had a 'peculiar redness of the whites of her eyes', said to be from constant weeping during the years of her troubles.)

The royal visitors went on to Corfe, to Encombe and to Weymouth. The Duchesse went even further. She visited Derbyshire, Birmingham and Malvern. Travelling under the name of Madame de Boigni, she drove to Bath (where Madame de Boigne suggests she gave birth to a daughter). During November the young widow also attended the opening of the Liverpool-Manchester railway, riding in the first carriage.

It was during these same autumn months, as the long grass faded and tangled with leaves, that the Duchesse found time to excavate the Five Marys. Did she stroll over to Chaldon from the castle after luncheon one afternoon? Or perhaps excavation took place at night by the light of flares - and to the hoot of an obligatory owl - with the Duchesse spiritedly directing the diggers in her *petit accent italien*. The occasion would be a perfect excuse for wearing breeches and doing some of the spadework herself.

Of the tumuli opened by the Duchesse, one was probably a bell, the other a bowl barrow. What she found in them must have been a shock, albeit a thrilling one. In the first barrow, at the bottom of a deep shaft, were two skeletons, one female and one male which had (wrote Charles Warne) 'by being placed in sitting positions, been adjusted to this their narrow, and last earthly tabernacle, whilst the antlers of a stag were severally placed on the shoulders of the skeletons respectively; i.e., on each of the four'. At the bottom of the second barrow sat another male form, also winged with antlers. Above it was a 'rudely manipulated urn', filled to overflowing with ashes and calcined bones. Such interments are rare, as again Warne does not fail to observe in his *Celtic Tumuli of Dorset*. They are, he observes, 'of somewhat an unusual character, inasmuch (if faithfully and correctly reported) as they differ so materially in the form of depositure generally recognised in Dorsetshire'.

Three stark figures, sitting upright, the blades of their shoulders fastened with antlers - like skeletal angels. The find is a singular one. Antlers have been found in other barrows in the county, at Bincombe, Swanage, Wimborne St. Giles, Winterborne Came and Winterborne St. Martin, but never arranged in quite this fashion. Like the flints, the antlers would be used to make tools and weapons - the deer which still stealthily graze the uplands were important to these early people.

But that juxtaposition of blade and antler? That could be seen as an accident of death, or simply as a rare survival. Or, given the nature of the Duchesse, there may have been some fanciful rearrangement of facts, or even of limbs. A more serious archaeologist, William Shipp, in his [third] edition of Hutchins's *Dorset* (1861), finds the skeletons interesting for yet another reason. The skulls, he confidently pronounces, were so low-browed 'as to indicate a very imperfect intellectual condition. It was also remarked that there were only 14 teeth in each jaw . . . evidently from pecularity of race, the jaw-bone comprising only this number of cavities or sockets. These facts, combined with other observations, led to the inference that the builders of the barrows under consideration were the primeval occupants of the South Dorset hills'.

The nineteenth century inhabitants of Chaldon, successors to these weird and short-toothed creatures, must have had their own thoughts about the goings-on in their village. They were the unrecorded witnesses (not for the last time) to the wild proceedings of a bunch of gentry, foreign at that - and, worst of all, French.

English coastal villages had often lived in fear of a French invasion, though not quite like this one. During the Napoleonic Wars, emergency measures had been taken to protect the Dorset headlands from foreign attack. Mary Frampton's brother, James, was appointed Captain of the Yeomanry from St Aldhelm's Head to Chaldon. Signal beacons were set up to warn of approaching danger: one of them was on the White Nose.

Measures like this can scarcely have allayed local fears at a time when invasion was expected daily, a time when, according to Thomas Hardy's story *A Tradition of Eighteen Hundred and Four*, it was possible to see, on the other side of the Channel, the weapons of the waiting French rank and file 'glittering in the sun like silver'. In this story a child is out at night watching his father's sheep on the lonely hills over Lulworth Cove. He is not afraid to be alone; 'the lack o' human beings at night made me less fearful than the sight of 'em'. So when one winter's night he sees two men, no more than twenty yards from his sheepfold, examining a map by the light of a lantern, he is naturally alarmed. One of these men, he discovers, is the dreaded 'Corsican ogre', Napoleon Bonaparte himself. The boy is close enough to see Boney's much-caricatured head, 'his short neck, his round yaller cheeks and

18

chin, his gloomy face, and his great glowing eyes'. The Emperor had been planning to land his troops in Lulworth Cove.

This haunting tale was an invention of Hardy's, but proved so precise an expression of common fears that it passed into local tradition. *The Life of Thomas Hardy* disingenuously relates how when the story was published its author was 'much surprised at people remarking to him: "I see you have made use of that well-known tradition of Napoleon's landing".' His own investigation showed that such a visit would in fact have been 'fatuous, and well nigh impossible. Moreover, that there had never existed any such improbable tradition'.

Such was the lingering force of the Napoleonic legend (and the craft of the storyteller) that this imaginary visit was long remembered. The corporeal arrival of his compatriot, the Duchesse de Berri, was soon forgotten, the excavated barrows her only souvenir. Marie-Caroline continued, though, to leave her mark on her beloved France, where she soon returned. (She had hoped to stay longer in Dorset, and was negotiating for the use of Came House, Dorchester, as her permanent residence, but so open a move, it was feared, might endanger the life of the young Henri, and the idea was abandoned.)

Some eighteen months later, in April 1832, the Duchesse landed secretly near Marseilles and headed for La Vendée, which had formerly been a Royalist stronghold. Marie-Caroline and her small but intrepid troop amused themselves on their journeying by selecting characters from Scott's novels and re-enacting their roles. Not surprisingly, they failed to drum up the support they required, and during November the Duchesse was arrested whilst hiding up a chimney in Nantes. The Vicomte de Chateaubriand, faithful admirer (and chronicler) of Marie-Caroline and now an increasingly reluctant actor in this wobbly drama, had been briefly detained as well. He noted with feeling the words of a fellow conspirator: '*faites pendre Walter Scott, car c'est lui qui est le vrai coupable*'.

Marie-Caroline, imprisoned in the fortress of Blaye, gave an individual twist to the plot when it was discovered that she was pregnant. Chateaubriand's *Illustre captive de Blaye* overnight became *la Magdelaine au diademe* who was jeopardising the Bourbon cause and her son's position as prince-in-waiting. Unperturbed as ever, the Duchesse amused herself by writing invisible messages in lemon juice to her two legitimate children, who were staying with their grandfather in Prague. The situation was only resolved by her hasty and secret marriage to a Sicilian count, Hector de

Lucchesi-Palli, who earned 100,000 francs for his pains, and the nickname 'St. Joseph' from the Parisian bourgeoisie. He took Marie-Caroline to Palermo, where her exile this time was permanent.

So the Duchesse was discredited, and the old graves desecrated. But up on the Five Marys a bold wind still blows through the hawthorns. It is rumoured that the barrows are haunted by a pair of lovers, disturbed bones, perhaps, who can occasionally be heard whispering.

Scratch the soil in Chaldon, and the ghosts will walk.

Ghosts at Chaldon Herring

Hush, my dear, hush!
Who are these that pass
Up shady lane?
Their feet don't brush
Any dew from the grass
And they are silent, too.

Hand in kind hand
Go some, and closelier linked
Another twain;
And others stand
As a-drouse, indistinct
Beneath the darkening boughs.

Ghosts, ghosts are these! -
Long-dead maidens, each
Beside her swain -
Between the trees
Pacing slow, without speech,
As they were wont to go.

Strange, some should choose
Thus their mouldered dears
To meet again,
Whom long misuse
Of marriage, taunts and tears,
And the slow grudge of age

Warped and estranged;
Sure, this place above

20

The Five Marys

All others fain
They'd leave unranged,
Lest a gaunt dead love
Them, like a dead child, haunt.

Ah, but not so
These who in true-love-knot
Their arms enchain.
Dead long ago
Are they all, and forgot
The life that held them thrall.

Nought now exists
Save fancies nursed apart.
And of all this train
Scarce one that trysts
With a seeming sweetheart
But walks beside a dream.

Sylvia Townsend Warner

10. Looking east to High Chaldon from West Chaldon.

11. Gilbert Spencer's frontispiece for *Fables* by T F Powys, 1929.

CHAPTER TWO

Theodore Powys at Beth Car

I do not know that I have seen a cottage so much like a doll's house as ours. An ugly one, too. But here in this haunted village, where even a hedgehog has his fancies a little ugliness may often hide more comfort than displeasure. I hate the dainty cottage of modern nicety; the build of ours is far more to my mind . . . Only see our cottage as it is, my dear friends. A doll's house made of bricks that once were red, and now by the damp sea mists have lost their colour; martins' nests under the eaves, in which the birds twitter at night as if they tell God's secrets. A half acre of grassy garden, the sound of trains when the wind is in the north, and the buzzing of inquisitive gnats is all we have to boast of.

T. F. Powys, 'Concerning Authors' Cottages'

When it was built, Beth Car was the first red-brick house in Chaldon, though since that time other suburban-looking structures have appeared in the village. The tradition is that the builder was Thomas Hardy's brother, Henry, and the architect Hardy himself. Certainly Beth Car is in the cramped style of Talbothays Lodge at West Stafford, or of Max Gate, the house the writer built for himself at Dorchester. All three buildings stand apart from their neighbours and all three, as Nikolaus Pevsner dryly wrote of Max Gate, have 'no architectural qualities whatsoever'.

David Garnett first visited Theodore Powys in 1922 and found the house 'the only eyesore in the lovely collection of long low white-washed cottages buried in deep thatch which formed the village, but it was fortunately out of sight, fronting the bare downs'. 'Ugly' and 'box-like' are recurring adjectives for any description of Beth Car, a fact its owner seemed to relish.

The front of the house, with its bay window, looks out and up to the hill of High Chaldon, a constant presence under various guises in Powys's writing, and a favourite object of his walks. Another often-visited spot was the churchyard, for which the house is most conveniently placed.

Beth Car is a Hebrew name meaning 'the house in the pasture', a title given to it by Theodore and painted in black letters on the white garden gate. In this garden, still surrounded by the grassland of a field called Chapel Banks, Powys cultivated potatoes and, he tells us, tied his fences up with string. He also planted trees: chestnut for quick growth and a weeping ash. He grew onions too - to give the ash 'something to weep for'. Later he more or less abandoned gardening as an unrewarding and exhausting struggle (he was never particularly strong). The rabbits triumphed and the hens, along with a couple of Indian runner ducks, won in a raffle at the Winfrith bazaar, scratched freely among the nettles. Other features of the house included a 'stick house' and - in the words of his friend, Sylvia Townsend Warner, a 'bleached and ricketty bench where on the first fine mornings of the year Theo likes to sit sunning himself, at the same time keeping a wary look-out for queen wasps'.

12. Beth Car and its weeping ash.

13. T F Powys and David Garnett with son Richard near Beth Car.

In her essay, Miss Warner gives a skittish account of Beth Car's beginnings. The Chaldon vicar, Joseph Staines Cope, she claims, ordered the house to be built for a curate, or possibly a gardener. Neither was forthcoming and as Mr Cope died - in 1902 - whilst the house was still unfinished, it remained in this state until taken by 'a retired rate-collector from Dorchester'. When the rate-collector removed to Swanage, Theodore bought the lease.

The deeds of sale show that Powys actually bought the leasehold of Beth Car in 1908 from a Mrs Kilby for £273.18.18. The house had previously been called 'The Nook'. Of this sum, £100 was borrowed from Louis Wilkinson, a family friend, and £93.18.18 was provided by Theodore's wife, Violet, raised from the sale of bonds left to her by her father, Joseph Dodds. Powys himself contributed £80, and the house was in his name.

Beth Car was not Theodore's first house in Chaldon. In 1904 when he moved from Studland with the aid of Mr Jacob's spring waggon, 'drawn by a blind white horse', he had taken Lilac Cottage, the end house of a terrace on the green, in the same row as the post office. It is an eighteenth century building, originally detached. Thatched and creepered, the cottage today has externally changed very little. On April 19, 1905, at the age of twenty-nine and described as a gentleman, Powys married a village girl, Violet Rosalie Dodds, daughter of 'Joseph Dodds, solicitor'. His brother Llewelyn was a witness. In Lilac Cottage in 1906 his elder son Theodore (usually called Dicky) was to be born.

14. By the village green. Lilac Cottage is at far end of terrace on the right.

Theodore's marriage has engendered much comment, some of it undoubtedly coloured by intellectual or social snobbery. The Powys family were after all, as they liked to remember, related to the Lords of Lilford, to (more nebulously) mythical Welsh princes and to the poets Cowper and Donne.

In his youth, Theodore had apparently been in love with Louis Wilkinson's sister, Christobel, a girl some six years his senior, who died of tuberculosis at the age of twenty-five. Louis Wilkinson also maintained that Theodore had fallen in love with two Wilkinson cousins 'in swift succession'. Later on, though, such women lost their appeal for Powys. In 1931 he told his brother Llewelyn, 'I don't want anything intellectual. I want little animals' roguery. I don't like ladies'.

From the portrait of women in his books this would seem to be true, but any inquiry into Theodore's feelings at an earlier stage remains a matter of conjecture. Francis Powys, his younger son, has suggested that Theodore may also have been in love with one of the four daughters of Mrs Stracey, whom he met whilst teaching English literature and history in two girls' schools in Eastbourne during 1902-3. Retrospectively, though, the mother was more important than any daughter. For years Mrs Stracey was Powys's only reader, admiring and encouraging him. By way of return, Theodore dedicated his *Interpretation of Genesis* to her, and selected her as godmother to Dicky and Francis.

But why Violet? Mark Holloway, a later visitor to Theodore and Violet, thought that she represented 'his chosen sphere of life: the village'. (Another visitor, Count Potocki, objected to Violet in a privately printed pamphlet for this very reason.) Theodore had consciously chosen Violet in much the same way as he had chosen Chaldon.

Violet was in any case a beautiful woman, as the early photographs show. She had long black hair, a rose-petal complexion and perfect legs. She was only eighteen when Theodore married her, and he was always attracted by young girls. The sculptor Stephen Tomlin was devoted to her; so was Sylvia Townsend Warner. 'It was Violet', she wrote, 'who came to open the door, Violet who I loved at first sight'. As she saw it, Theodore had chosen wisely. Violet was the life-line between her husband and the village, returning from the Chaldon post office, or from a trip to Dorchester on the bus, or reading aloud bits of local news from the *Dorset Echo*.

Observant, speculative, credulous, unaffectedly interested in her neighbours, naturally talking the local dialect yet just enough removed from it to have an ear for its idioms, and with a memory ramifying into every local pedigree and bygone event and oddity, she was an inestimably good purveyor - with the crowning merit of remaining unconscious of it ... Under any circumstances, TFP would have been a writer; but I suspect his bent towards theology and contemplation would have kept him writing about God and Theodore Francis Powys if Violet had not drawn his attention to humanity.

Years later, Miss Warner was still championing Violet. As she wrote to Llewelyn's widow, Alyse Gregory, in 1967, 'It was Violet who kept his neck out of the noose. Not only did she incessantly serve him: she supplied him. Her faith in him, her blind chivalrous trust in his genius, was the essential vitamin in his life. With her he felt safe, was at his ease and was entertained'.

In her reply, Alyse, perhaps too intellectually austere to warm spontaneously to Violet, reservedly agreed.

Violet could be feckless, possessive, malicious, jealous, she never forgot a slight - nor, equally a kindness - she could also work herself to the bone to help almost anyone who was in trouble - she almost killed herself over those old aunts - she was very generous, and entertaining as well, courageous, she never spent any money on herself.., of course she had very little intelligence but for someone with Theodore's propensity towards melancholy I think she was good . . .

The marriage was to last to the end. Their adopted daughter, Theodora ('Susie'), a generation younger than her brothers, observed that they were devoted to one another 'in a baffled sort of way'. If in his dependence Theodore had felt contempt for his wife and daughter, as Alyse Gregory had suspected, then she had not been aware of it. And judging by the wildly disordered state of her life after her husband's death, Violet was equally reliant on Theodore's steady and cautious approach to life's practicalities.

For Violet, life with Theodore could not have been easy. She must have thought she had made a 'good' marriage and her expectations would have been high, especially after the move to Beth Car, a large house for the village (though comprising a series of small rooms). It was described in the Estate Catalogue of 1929 when the Weld family attempted to sell off Chaldon as having Dining Room, Drawing Room, Kitchen, Pantry, 3 Bedrooms, an outside coal shed and 2 roods of land. There was also - uncatalogued - a poltergeist.

These were the bare facts. Francis Powys, born and brought up in Beth Car, remembered harsher details. Very little meat was eaten, only the occasional hen or rabbit. Many a meal was made on bread and treacle: a favourite with most of the Powys family. The house had no running water (the estate tap water extended only to cattle) and they had to go into the village for a well. Also, Chaldon was a village much plagued by rats, of which Beth Car had its share. Great quantities of poison were used in an attempt to keep the rats down.

Village life was plain and sometimes hard. The lanes, a mix of mud and chalk, were slow and well-trodden. Smoke came mazily from the chimneys, wood-fragrant and acrid. Washing flapped, or dismally dripped, from clothes-lines in cottage gardens. The barking of dogs was a constant irritant, like a ticklish, unsuppressed cough. 'A dog barks here too at night . . . it always barks like that, it belongs to Farmer Tod', Theodore wrote to his brother John in 1917.

Money was scarce in the village; it was also scarce at Beth Car, and a continual worry to Theodore, who was struggling to get a grasp on his financial affairs. 'Money', he wrote in a later letter to John, 'when it buys me sugar and tea and brown bread I can understand, but when it gets further than that point, it becomes a thing not so simple'. Nor was Theodore so simple. Although he genuinely feared that his younger sisters were literally eating up his share of his father's inheritance by their appetites, he had also shown, during his brief career as a Suffolk farmer, that he was capable of keeping the books. The innocent ballad-like view of wealth presented in his novels is that of the poor countryman - and also, partly, of himself. Powys, like the villagers, experienced poverty. Some of them were far poorer, but only for him, perhaps, was it such a humiliating state: he had known a very different way of life. The poverty knocking in his books does so with a true echo. In this Theodore was able to share the life of the people amongst whom he lived.

15. Theodore and Violet Powys.

The scarcity of money at Beth Car was what Violet found difficult to accept. The early years together, especially around the time Francis was born in 1909 were, Theodore wrote, some of the happiest times in his life. His sister Katie's journal details many a cheerful and contented visit. But when war broke out in 1914, it was part-mirrored by the disturbances at Beth Car. Powys was much troubled by the unprecedented slaughter in Europe and half-guilty, half-relieved at his repeated rejection on medical grounds for conscription. He wanted to be a writer, but so far had only published *An Interpretation of Genesis* in 1907, which he had paid for at least partly himself, appalling Violet by the cost. He relied on the allowance of £100 a year given to each married member of the family by his father, the vicar of Montacute (the unmarried children receiving £60), and by further financial help from family and friends. During this time John Cowper Powys sent Theodore £1 a week from the hard-earned proceeds of his lectures in America.

Matters seem to have reached their lowest ebb around 1917-18 by which time Theodore, wearied by Violet's complaints about money, had become attracted to her half-sister, Georgina, who lived in the village with their mother and Violet's step-father Jack Jacobs (whom Violet disliked). Theodore wrote about her in *Georgina: A Lady* and as Ivy Gale in *Amos Lear*, both of which remain unpublished. As a portrait, *Georgina* suggests that she was pretty, a bit spoilt, independent and high-spirited. Ivy is altogether a poorer creature, but her love of finery and concern that her clothes should not become stained, may be characteristics borrowed from Georgie. Both girls are, like Georgie, enthusiastic about soldiers. In reality, Georgina was an unsatisfactory consolation, as is made plain in a letter Theodore wrote to John in December 1917.

But I am beaten my dear what with Violet eternally nagging indoors, and the dread of thing[s] happening, and that I don't seem able to bear - to Georgie out of doors. Or more likely at her parents . . . and of course I have held Georgie so present - so very present for 10 years. As though she - ignorant foolish and selfish as she is - was worth holding . . .

The stamp of despair is on many of Theodore's letters at this period. In 1918 he wrote to John, 'I keep on telling Violet that her sons at the Prep is not that glory and honour enough ... I am beaten in . . I daresay it is poverty and fretting about little things that has done it'. Never easy, his carefully chosen life had turned into a trap. In another letter he wrote, 'Good Lord I envy everyone'. His brothers Llewelyn and John were both in America and enjoying, in his embittered imagination at least, a much more extravagant existence.

> Lulu and Jack dance naked on the sands
> of California but so do not I.

The sentiments are typical of this period of Theodore's life. So, it might be said, is the syntax, the curiously-inverted sentences which are a result of Theodore's reading of the Bible, particularly the Old Testament. For years his commentary on Genesis remained his only published work, but manuscripts still exist of commentaries on almost all the books of the Old Testament, written about the same time as Genesis around 1906-8. From the New Testament, there are only manuscripts for the gospels of Mark and John, along with John's Epistles.

Descended from five generations of clergymen, three on his father's side and two on his mother's, Theodore had been brought up on the Bible and was an intensely religious child. He and his mother, a devout Christian, would sit for hours in silent contemplation. 'Religion is the only subject I know anything about', he wrote in *Soliloquies of a Hermit*. Together with the works of Bunyan, the Bible is the most conspicuous influence on his fiction, and affected all three of the brothers who became writers. 'My brothers and I,' John Cowper Powys wrote, '- it was what we all had in common - had acquired, out of our readings from earliest childhood a deep earthy response to the Authorized Version of the Bible'. The Bible, with its pure English, uncomplicated expression, and limited range of ideas, made an ideal starting-point for Theodore.

In *Genesis*, Powys's mouthpiece Zetetes accuses the Lawgiver, 'Thou dost not follow the story of the old poets, for thou alterest the story where thou wilt'. By the time of his second published work *Soliloquies of a Hermit* in 1916, Theodore does more than that: he turns orthodox Christianity on its head. He is, he writes, without a belief, as 'a belief is too easy a road to God'. Yet he is subject still to 'the moods of God' and is a receptacle for them. This makes him one of the priest class. Most other people are governed by one mood alone, usually 'the getting mood'. Such people are immortal; immortality is one of the things they grab after.

Immortality is for Powys an undesirable state. He is a priest, and the priests will die. While they are alive, their lives are difficult, fear-haunted. They cannot escape the fear of God which is everywhere: 'the very winds bring it; it comes out of the stones'.

Theodore emerges from his own account as a tormented and unhappy creature, one whom the moods of God have hunted out remorselessly. If he had come to Chaldon in search of peace, then he has not yet succeeded in finding it - 'In the most quiet places the moods of God rend and tear the heart'.

Sometimes he glimpses how life might be, if God were kinder to him. 'It is one of the most curious feelings that I know, this one of being on the side of God, on the safe side'. He sees too, from his distance, the beauty of his own country world.

And we watched, in the valley beneath us, tiny children running to school beside a little blue trickle of water, and large gulls were washing and flapping their wings in the water. The children called to them and waved their arms, and the gulls rose and spread like snowflakes over the valley, and the children ran on, holding each other's hands and singing.

This aspect of the book had already been sounded out in *Cottage Shadows*, an unpublished novel from about 1911. The narrator of this story, a much more orthodox Christian than Theodore called Francis Wingrave, has become disillusioned with his marriage and with village life. He was lured from the town by the beauty of the countryside, but the cottage shadows have soon taught him that 'man is irrevocably alone'.

A similar disillusionment is recorded in *Soliloquies*. With such scenes of beauty all around him, it is easy to see how the hermit used to believe that 'all the poetry of the world came from the cottage'. Now he sees how the people 'slave and toil and tear at each other with the claws of the beast' in their attempt to use work as an escape from God - and it is even worse in the towns, as he is to show in *Hester Dominy*. Not all types of work, though, are so reviled; some are acceptable to the hermit.

I see an old cart trundling along filled with turnips, going about a mile an hour; I see a rabbit-catcher half-hidden in a rabbit hole, quietly wondering where to set his next snare, and turning at last his slow steps to the inn to exchange a rabbit for beer.

Powys too is happiest when mending his garden railings, or some such homely task. He is fond of old familiar objects like his chair, or a broken roller in a field. People who do not understand this sometimes smile at him. They 'point at your thistles and count your nettles, [and] wonder why you do not keep fowls, or why you keep a row of five broken buckets by your back door'.

The tone is defensive; again and again in *Soliloquies*, Theodore is justifying his chosen existence. The book had emerged from John's idea that the six brothers should write a joint confession (then a popular genre). John's and Llewelyn's were published together as *Confessions of Two Brothers* and

Theodore's separately (originally in America in 1916) as *Soliloquy of a Hermit*. Perhaps aware that odious comparisons might be made, Theodore is sounding the defensive note - defensive and intensely self-conscious. In Chapter 13, the liveliest section of the book, Powys parodies himself as Mr Thomas, presenting himself as he might be seen through the eyes of that most dreadful of creatures, an urban gentleman down for the shooting. The result is gently comic.

Mr Thomas is married, and he digs in his garden. He looks rather like a landscape artist who has spent ten summers in trying to draw an old footbridge, two willow trees, and a cow, and could never finish his picture because the cow would never lie down.

Yet in *Soliloquies* Powys does not claim to have chosen the simple life. Social conventions, like religious ones, have been inverted. To Theodore the simple life is 'the life of motor-cars, of divorces, of monkey dances'. His own life is more difficult to achieve and is grossly misunderstood, even by the villagers. 'I own a cottage, therefore my value to the clown is exactly the value of my cottage, plus the value of my overcoat and the value of my boots'. This is a serious undervaluation.

And feeling as I do the very movements of God, I do not like to be treated as a poor man who cannot afford a day labourer to dig his garden.

The hermit can be crabby. The tone is one of affronted dignity, an unusually subjective one for Powys, and indicative of the difficulties of his life at this time. Despite such rash patches, though, this peculiar document can be regarded as an initial statement of Powys's beliefs, which are to reappear more coherently and fully in the novels and short stories. Unsurprisingly, his philosophy is shown at its most jaundiced in a novel contemporary with *Soliloquies, Mr Tasker's Gods*.

The book is set in the village of Shelton, one of a clutch of villages with different names and varying functions, all modelled, with the exceptions of Tadnol and Mockery Gap which are topographically separate, on Chaldon Herring. In *Mr Tasker*, Shelton in its setting is Chaldon to the life - a village locked in a stone ring of hills, the sea to the south, the heath to the north, the outside world a carrier's trip away, or a short ride on the South-Western Railway.

Recognisable too are the tone and style of the writing (as they are in much earlier attempts at fiction, like *The Snow Queen* of 1902) and the dramatic control of the opening chapter, where the two vicarage maids are kept awake by the drunken disturbances of Mr Tasker returning to his dairy. Soon, though, the overloaded plot leaves the novel in as much mud as the greedy gods of Mr Tasker: his pigs. Powys had yet to learn mastery of his material - and he knew it.

Through inexperience and a certain gloomy desperation, Powys lays on the blood and gore with relish. It is an odd dish. The vicar's youngest son is kicked to death, the carter dies of a bite from his old dog, Mr Tasker's father

16. Illustration by Ray Garnett for *Mr Tasker's Gods,* 1925.

is eaten by the pigs. The country people live hard and brutal lives and rejoice in one another's misfortune. The pleasant, rustic appearance of the village, as seen by the visitor, belies the truth of the 'two in one, beast and man'. There is no hope of improvement or redemption. The only outside aid comes in the resourceful but unlikely form of Rose Netley, a social worker, and Mr Malden, her German chess-playing companion.

The main interest of the book lies in the characters, who are differently presented from those of the later novels. Although Mr Tasker (a man most definitely in the 'getting mood' so condemned by Powys the hermit) is a predecessor of Farmer Mew in *The Left Leg*, and Mrs Fancy, the voyeuristic landlady anticipates Mrs Vosper in *Mr Weston's Good Wine*, they are more naturalistically drawn than their successors. Two characters, Henry Turnbull and Henry Neville, are critical self-portraits of the younger and older Theodore. The younger Henry, having 'never got beyond the third form of a rather poor preparatory school', is shipped off to Canada to become a farmer. On his return he grew a beard - although unlike Theodore he was not heard to address it as a separate person - 'and read curious, old-fashioned little brown books, books written by old forgotten Church Fathers who thought like angels'. He is regarded as a near-idiot by his family, and is certainly weak, although gentle and kindly. The older Henry has a face 'more strong than clever; it had indeed none of those hard, ugly lines, those examination lines, that mark the educated of the world. His beard and hair were grey, and his heart, could it have been seen was greyer still; and no wonder, for he had found out what human unkindness was'.

The war, his lack of success as a writer, and the subsequent withdrawal of loving support by Violet, on which he depended throughout his life, his poverty and (by no means least) the toothache with which he was tormented, all contributed to Theodore's depression. What caused him to look so grim, wrote Sylvia Townsend Warner, was '*his teeth*, which were poisoning him and making his life a misery'. A letter to John confirms this medieval horror.

I have tried to have some of my teeth out. About half. I can't face the rest of it though. Bloody Blasted Damned Coward that I am.

The origin of the mood is harder to trace. Sylvia Townsend Warner thought it began on the Suffolk farm, believing that there was 'some sort of a crisis there, some plunge into the pit which left a black mark on him'. Theodore never wrote nor talked about it, but 'he did once intimate that he had known an extreme melancholy there, as well as the mortification of being cheated by a bad bailiff; and there are shadows of it in *Mr Tasker's Gods*'.

Disillusionment sours and distorts the novel, though running through it is an exhilarating thread of anarchy. Of the clergymen in the book, most are lecherous, idle hypocrites, betrayers of their sacred trust, and sure candidates for immortality. The God of the vicarage is 'a remarkably easy god to please'. Bishops, policemen, even churchwardens are satirised; so too is the coroner. As a young man on a visit to friends at Cambridge, Theodore had dismissed the Church, Navy, Army and Bar as 'liars, murderers and thieves'. In *Mr Tasker* he is still of the same opinion. Mostly, though, the author seems overburdened by his material and quite unable to control the tone - often to ludicrous effect. While choosing a place in unconsecrated ground to bury the body of Henry Neville, killed by his own hand (an act condoned by the author) after succumbing to a hereditary disease, the diggers trample on some 'shaky wooden crosses' marking the graves of infants. Later, having side-stepped an unwieldy stack of omens, young Henry is kicked to death and his murderer devoured by pigs all in one hectically bloody chapter. After this, the hapless reader cannot be surprised at Powys's inclusion amongst the parodied in *Cold Comfort Farm*.

The hare died in the gin. The owl tore out the bowels of the rat. In the heath cottage, Molly covered the face of the dead Henry.

So the chapter ends. Powys might be trying to outdo Hardy in the grim fatalism of his tale. He comes nearest to Hardy in his first novels, in *Mr Tasker's Gods* and in *Mark Only*, written some five years later. In *Mr Tasker*, for instance, the scene in which the death of the Rev. Hector Turnbull is slowly realised by his apprehensively curious Portstown landlady resembles Hardy's account of the death of Alec in *Tess of the d'Urbervilles*.

Mrs Fancy had never in her life felt a silence so full of meaning, as the silence that followed the fall. Nothing moved in the house, nothing moved anywhere. She could hardly at that moment believe that anything had been going on at all. Had she, after all, been dreaming? - she might have fallen asleep in her kitchen chair - or had her lodgers flown up the chimney like bats?

Like Hardy, Theodore knew the lives of the country people. He had been a farmer, was one no longer. He knew about agriculture, knew the feel of the work and its rhythms, as his daughter Theodora relates.

He told me about the deep Suffolk clay and how after ploughing it would lie like boulders in the field, almost impossible to break with roller or harrow. He described the autumn ploughing, the weight of the plough as you swing it at the end of the furrow, the snort and stamping of the team and the tossing of the great proud heads as the horses kept the furrow straight .

Theodore observed the work of the village people and admired their painfully-acquired, undervalued skills. In December 1945 he wrote to his sister Katie about Frank Wallis, publican and roadmender, who had recently died.

I have been thinking a great deal more about Mr Wallis than about Christmas a festival that I always wish over . . . I remember so well . . . how I met so often Mr Wallis breaking stones . . . . - and how I always wondered how he could just hit the flint right. He would not allow there was much art in it. He had those dark glasses on. For hours and hours he would crack those flints as easily as God Almighty will one day, and perhaps very soon, crack this world and the little splinters will fly .

In *Cottage Shadows*, written thirty-five years before, Powys is already noting how, when moving furniture, the men handled it 'with that cautious tenderness that simple people always use towards the meanest article of cottage

17. Ray Garnett's woodcut for T.F.Powys's short story *The Key of the Field*, 1930.

furniture'. This, he suggests, 'may have its origin in the countryman's firm belief that all material things connected with, or made by man, are spiritually alive'. Such material things are alive to Theodore also, and are used for the only kind of work he feels able to admire: plain hard labour with pick or plough.

Mark Only is a ploughman, though, thanks to an accident that left him partially-sighted, 'no good worker'. Ploughing on the hill above the village is probably the most important part of his life. 'He had always, since he had first been trusted by his father with horses and a plough, gloried in the drawing of a furrow'. Powys described the slow, painstaking nature of the work, the plough disturbing mouse and hare, lark and mole. Despite his increasing troubles (which include the final onset of blindness) Mark continues to climb the hill and patiently to do his work.

The model Theodore used for the character of Mark was Violet's stepfather, Jack Jacobs. Like Mark, Jack Jacobs (it is said) gradually lost his inheritance to his brother. The people of Chaldon were to provide much of the matter for Theodore's books, usually contributing one characteristic (or skill) rather than a complete character. Two people disliked by Theodore were Mr Diment the West Chaldon farmer before 1928 and his idle son, Bobby, who used to steal apples from the Beth Car trees. Village girls working as servants at West Chaldon had to take care to lock themselves into their rooms at night to escape the attentions of Bobby. Farmer Diment, the story goes, employed three lunatic men as cheap labour who would lie in wait and bite anyone they encountered walking down the lane. The middle farm, Grange Farm, was in the hands of Mr Todd (Mr Childs had Vicarage, the third farm). Todd used to dump his dead animals, horses and cows, in the Rat's Valley, so that for a while it became known as Dead Horse Valley. There were, too, in the village men like Jack Trim, layabout and cripple, who had a (perhaps unmerited) reputation for womanising. Cruel or mean farmers, feckless sons, easy-going labourers, all take their places in Powys's fiction, simplified maybe, but not necessarily exaggerated.

Local happenings were also used. According to Francis Powys, a notorious village incident forms the basis of the scene in *Mark Only* where the child is christened. Here, the villagers are gathered in the church for Mark Andrews' baptism. The font is leaking, and in the bottom, distracting the parson's attention, is a centipede.

'What name?' he asked crossly.
'Mark,' replied Mr Andrews, and then added a little louder, 'Mark only.'
Mr Hayball looked into the font. By putting his fingers to the bottom discreetly and warily, he might by good luck avoid the centipede.
'Mark Only, I baptize thee in the name of the Father and of the Son, and of the Holy Ghost'.

Mark's beginnings are ill-fated, so is his end. The church lane in Chaldon is said to be haunted by a black dog; the lanes of Dodderdown are roamed by spectral hounds which 'could still be heard if one listened long enough on a windy or a gloomy day. Dying folk were always sure to hear the scamper of their feet in the lanes, even though the windows of the cottage were fast-closed; and the healthy even, and especially those who had more than an ordinary fear of death, were troubled at certain times by the sound of these dogs running'. They were the 'biting dogs' who came for Mark's ten-year-old sister as she lay dying of scarlet fever. On the last day of his life Mark follows the sound of them up the hill, where he dies in the snow. 'The dogs had him, the good dogs'.

Nature is very red in tooth in Powys's novels, and biting held for him a morbid fascination. There were plenty of sharp-toothed rats in the village to stir these feelings. Not that Theodore had a particular horror of rats; to him they were more of a rather nasty memento mori. Sylvia Townsend Warner tells of Theodore coming hastily back from a walk and remarking, 'I heard a noise in the hedge. I said to myself, It's only a rat. But then I thought, Who made that rat?'

Humans too can bite and often do. *Mark Only* is a better-constructed novel than *Mr Tasker*, but at times it lurches out of control. Once Mark's brother James has seduced Mark's wife and made her his servant, his desires run in all directions. His eye falls on the maidservant, Emmie, whom he watches with 'a hungry look, as though he wondered which to bite next'.

Emmie is belatedly rescued from the clutches of James and of the evil Tulk, a figure as misshapen as Dickens's Quilp, by the outside, bumbling agency of Mr Thomas the sweep (Theodore in half-disguise). No one else even attempts to intervene. The rector of Dodderdown, Mr Hayball, does not offer the village any spiritual leadership - like the rector of Norbury in Powys's *Black Bryony*, written in 1917, he is kindly but ineffectual. Hayball is mainly interested in 'limestones, clays and marls' along with old stones, while the Norbury parson, Rev. Crossley, is absorbed in his book of gospel commentaries. Anyway, it would not occur to any of the villagers to seek their help; Mark Only is Mark alone.

By the time *Mark Only* was completed in 1922, Powys had still not published any fiction (although interest had been shown in *Mr Tasker's Gods*). He kept on writing day by day, as the major part of his routine.

Theodore was a creature of habit. 'Powys believes in monotony', he wrote in 1925. 'He is happy when he does the same thing every day. Writes from 11 to 1.30. Walks nearly always the same path in the afternoon, goes by the

Inn to the Hill'. He wrote in the front bay window, from which he could see High Chaldon, and any approaching visitors. On his walks he would take a rest, sitting on a little waterproof sheet and smoking one cigarette. Sometimes he would gather driftwood on the cliffs, above the sea which was so important to him. Except for his birthplace in Shirley, Derbyshire, Theodore had never lived more than a good walking distance from the sea - in Dorchester and Montacute, at school in Aldeburgh and farming at Sweffling in Suffolk, in Eastbourne, Studland and Chaldon. Francis Wingrave, the hero of the largely autobiographical *Cottage Shadows*, chose a place 'within easy reach of the sea', which was also 'far too plain and simple to attract any common visitor'. Ideally for Wingrave, the sea should be within hearing, coming over the low hills. There is 'a vast melancholy' in its sound. 'But this melancholy was the kind of sensation he desired to have near him'.

Theodore's life was always a plain one. 'Restrict your wants', he wrote, 'and life simplifies itself miraculously'. His work was central to it, shaping his life. The reverse also holds true - due to his writing methods, the chapters of his early books are end-stopped, rarely flowing on. He also read, thoroughly and widely, ancient and modern, and was largely self-taught. His books are full of subtle literary allusion, garnered from his reading. Unlike that of the rest of his brothers, his education had been a haphazard affair, as he described to his sister Gertrude in 1941.

My education!!
I was at Dorchester Grammar School in the lowest form taken there by Aunt Philippa . . . I think I was there 3 terms, during most of one of those terms I was ill of jaundice. Then I went to the Prep for 3 terms. By that time I was 12 years old. I had measles one of those terms and went to Weymouth afterwards to stay with Cousin Mary and I suppose Grandmother. I remember the wonderful fresh eggs and toast. Father taught me after that in front of the study window that you cannot look out of . . . Before Lucy was born I was sent to Aldeburgh - with a cricket bat that had black string tied round it near the bottom. I was treated with respect owing to that bat and owing to my being then 14 years old . . . I was there 4 or 5 terms, and left just before I was 16. There ended my education.

His later studies more than compensated for his lack of formal education. He read methodically as he did everything, in his neat and ordered way. He was 'finicky as a cat' - except in dress, which was habitually untidy.

He was not a traveller, increasingly less so. Travel was upsetting, and also pointless. Once when he went to meet John Cowper Powys, his wife Margaret and son Littleton at Wool railway station, the train was late. On arrival, John expressed concern at the delay, and Theodore replied, 'I might just as well wait here as anywhere else. The end is bound to come if we wait long enough'.

As a young man, Theodore had travelled to Chinon, to visit the birthplace of his admired Rabelais, and he may also have been to Ireland. In 1923 he made his last visit to London, when he and Violet went to see their son Dicky off to Africa. He never went as far again. He wrote of himself, 'Since a visit to London in 1923 he has steadfastly refused to travel so far afield. Contenting himself with an occasional journey to either Dorchester or Weymouth, where he spends most of the day, anyhow at the latter place, "looking at the sea and wishing he were home again!" '

This local journey was made on 'the very ponderous 'bus, that labours up and down the Dorset hills, and takes over an hour to travel ten miles'. Until his death in 1933, this vehicle was owned by Mr Goult. It was a wooden Dennis bus, with solid tyres. Afterwards, Mr Webb ran the bus and taxi business, washing his car in the river. The Webb family still run the Chaldon buses today.

The bus, and the carrier's van, were lifelines to small villages in the early part of the century. Before the First World War the van was horse-drawn, built like a square covered waggon and lined with two wooden benches. It was often packed with people who, whenever there was a hill - as there so often was - would have to get out and walk. On the way home the van would probably have to be lit, by carriage lamps with candles in them.

Soon after 1914 motor buses made their first appearance. They were the only form of motor in which Theodore considered travelling, as he regarded cars with trepidation and dislike. On being taken for a drive one evening, he observed how the windscreen became splattered with the tiny bodies of insects. 'To motor by night', he remarked, 'must be agony to a moth-collector'. It was a mild reproof; he would not wish to appear ungrateful. Of motors and motoring he wrote, 'A Journey in a motor car is the most tiring experience in the world . . . When I am tired all I feel fit to do is to stroke a cat'.

Keeping such distractions to the minimum, Theodore went on writing, and when his work began to be accepted, had drawerfuls of material in reserve. His understandable eagerness to be accepted is shown in his willingness to allow the revision of *Mr Tasker*, confessing that the chapters could as easily be reshuffled as not. Then, too, when David Garnett pointed out after reading *Black Bryony* that the plant is more commonly white, and that the shape of the leaf was wrong, Theodore replied,

41

'Heart-shaped' would be a truer description of Black Bryony, but I couldn't use it because it doesn't sound nicely. My Black Bryony leaves are vine shaped. I don't see why I shouldn't create a leaf as well as a story. It is a little unfortunate of course that to the best of my remembrance I have never seen a vine. And so I don't know what a vine shaped leaf looks like. But I can't alter it now.

He was reluctant to alter the name in case it endangered his chance of publication. (And, though he does not say so, change would also ruin a pointlessly unpleasant pun, as Bryony is the name of a baby burnt to death in a rectory fire.)

By the time of this correspondence, Theodore's work was beginning to be published. Like the rescue of his characters, it had needed outside aid. His rescuer was a young man presently embarking on a career as a sculptor. His name was Stephen Tomlin.

Stephen (Tommy) Tomlin discovered the village of Chaldon Herring whilst on a walking tour during Easter, 1921. He returned to stay there in the autumn, when he first met Theodore. He was deeply impressed by him, as people generally were, and told his friend Sylvia Townsend Warner, 'There is a most remarkable man living just beyond the village. He is a sort of hermit, and he has a very fine head. He reads Dostoievsky . . . [and] I believe he writes'.

Soon he was reading some of these writings and was impressed by them, too, encouraging Theodore in his work. Theodore wrote to John that 'Mad Tom says I am only just beginning to get my right medium'. 'Mad Tom' was a man well-qualified to appreciate Powys's work. He had a highly intelligent and analytical mind. His father was to become a judge, and Tommy inherited his forensic abilities. At school, if the portrait of him as Billy Williams in Sylvia Townsend Warner's *A Garland of Straw* is to be believed, he was 'successful, popular, and unhappy'. He went up to New College, Oxford, in 1919 and became a close friend of J. M. Barrie's beloved ward, Michael Llewelyn Davies. Michael's death by drowning caused Tomlin to suffer a complete nervous collapse.

Tomlin left Oxford, it seems, without completing his degree, and went instead to study sculpture under Frank Dobson. He wanted to become 'a simple artisan', and certainly showed no little talent for the work. His intensely-felt sympathies for other people made him capable of capturing their likenesses, just as he was able to help them by 'interpreting life so as to create for their benefit something intelligible and hopeful', leaving no energy left for himself. Tomlin could well understand Theodore's own melancholy,

42

then at its greatest. In 1967, Sylvia Townsend Warner discussed this in a letter to Alyse Gregory: 'when Theodore showed him those exercise books in pale ink which were lying unpublished and uncomprehended [he] knew the reason for the stern, tortured countenance'.

Soon, too, he was sculpting that unmistakeable head. All that remains of the sculpture (as of so much of Tomlin's work) is a photograph. In a letter to Theodore of January 1923, Tommy wrote, 'My portrait of you fell irrevocably to pieces on the way up, alas!'

18. Stephen Tomlin with his head of Theodore Powys, 1923.

Such disasters apart, Tomlin's work benefitted from his visits to Chaldon. Bea Howe, who knew both Tommy and Sylvia in their early days, has suggested that the landscape of the Chaldon valley is better suited to a sculptor than a painter. Here and there, the flinty backbone of the hills shows through the turf, the skull is very close to the skin. Chaldon is a place of bone, a place of stones, and as such appealed to the sculptor in Tomlin.

Tommy easily felt at home in the village, as did the person to whom he showed Theodore's work, Sylvia Townsend Warner. They, along with David Garnett, were instrumental in bringing about the publication of Powys's fiction, a fact acknowledged by Theodore in his dedication to the three stories in *The Left Leg*, published in 1923. In a letter to Sylvia, Powys elaborated on this dedication.

Each story is dedicated to a person. The first, the God head, is you - the second David the Dove - the third. . . . to Tom the son of Man.

In her first letter to Theodore, Miss Warner had asked if she might read *Mr Tasker's Gods*. She received a reply on a page torn from a copybook 'with copper-plate sentiments occurring at regular intervals down the ruled page'. (There was something of a shortage of paper in the village. Mary Jane Legg, who presided over the post-office and shop for more than thirty years, sold 'all the necessities of village life, such as buttons, candles, liquorice, india-rubber spouts for broken tea-pots and ointment against lice', small items for which small change was given in pins. When it came to writing material the choice was between notepaper, floral or plain, and regulation school exercise-books. Frugally, Theodore wrote notes on the backs of envelopes, in his children's notebooks, on old bills - anywhere.)

When Sylvia came to Chaldon a few months later, the meeting was immediately successful. If Theodore was a hermit, he was an unfailingly courteous one, and Violet was famous for her 'splendid teas'. Sylvia loved them both, and they returned her feeling. In 1924 Theodore wrote to Sylvia, 'Violet and I talk about you with more affection than we do of anyone else in the world except our children'. To John Cowper Powys he wrote describing Sylvia as 'a wonderful person with a biting mind . . . we are both very fond of her'. By 1926, Sylvia is offering to buy a bed with a Vi-Spring mattress (as used by King George) for Theodore and Violet. By 1930 she is signing her letters 'your daughter Sylvia'.

Financially, too, these were happier times, as Theodore told John. 'We can now afford pickled onions to our supper. There are also sticks in our woodshed, and what is more wonderful *Coal*'. When the Rev. Charles Powys died in 1923 he left each of his children £3,000. For the moment at least, Theodore's financial troubles were over. He was beginning to be published, he had acquired some new and well-loved friends. He also began to receive, for someone of his retiring nature, rather too many visitors.

Tomlin, Warner and Garnett were not alone in their admiration of Theodore. Liam O'Flaherty, whilst living 'in a tent in a damp spot at the back of an old vicarage' and writing his novel *The Informer* had 'many lengthy discussions' with Powys, and gave a highly favourable review to *Mr Tasker's Gods*. Valentine Ackland wrote that she came to 'revere T. F. Powys profoundly' and looked on him as 'a blend of Socrates, William Blake and God the Father'. The painter Carrington noted in her diary that 'Mr Powys seems without a fault. He was so beautiful good and gracious.'

Another visitor was T. E. Lawrence, about whom Theodore wrote to John, 'Violet and I like him he is very mild and modest', though on his first visit, Theodore had mistaken him for a tax-collector. He would come over to Beth Car from his Clouds Hill cottage on his motorcycle, which he called Boanerges. He would time himself on the journey, aiming each time to beat his own record for the trip. This apparently did not go down well with some of the villagers. 'A-tearin' up an' down lane on tick screechin' thing; gome rain, gome shine, gome day, gome night, gome Zundays, gome weekdays, 'tees all alike to he - an' 'tees unzeemly.'

Calmer visitors arrived in the spring of 1929, when the writers H.E.Bates and Rhys Davies, along with Charles Lahr of the *New Coterie,* made a literary trip to Chaldon. This was probably the occasion on which Lahr presented Theodore with a copy of Charles Duff's *A Handbook on Hanging*, with the inscription: '(This book might come in useful when you hang one of your characters.)'

More alarming to Theodore was the visit of Lady Ottoline Morrell, who originally wrote inviting him to Garsington Manor. Prolonged negotiations on the subject came to nothing, and in September 1924 Lady Ottoline descended on Beth Car. Theodore politely but steadfastly declined to make a return visit, even refusing the offer of an arrangement to go and see Thomas Hardy in Dorchester. On October 1st 1924 Theodore wrote, 'Certainly everyone who leaves East Chaldon does go into darkness . . . I haven't been to Max Gate, I believe Mrs Hardy keeps dogs who might mistake me for an American'. Nevertheless he did eventually risk a visit to Hardy, telling Lady Ottoline, 'I enjoyed my visit . . . to Max Gate. What a wonderful old man. And she was kind too'. Afterwards Florence Hardy wrote thanking Theodore for undertaking 'that long journey from East Chaldon'. She added: 'I do wish that for once my husband had abandoned his rule of never praising people's work to their face, and had told you how interested he has been in your novels - which I have read to him. He fully realises their power, and your compelling style - Only I fear he does side with the reviewers in thinking you do make country people a bit blacker than they really are . . .'

Visitors to Beth Car were invariably struck by Theodore Powys. He was a man of imposing appearance. When David Garnett first saw him he was a 'grey-haired, elderly, heavily-built man with a big head and powerful rugged features'. Under bushy eyebrows he had sharp grey eyes which 'summed one up; he was a moralist and a shrewd critic of men'. 'Elderly', Theodore was not: when Garnett met him he was approaching fifty. He might, though, have liked the epithet. Sylvia Townsend Warner noted that he imposed himself as elderly whilst still middle-aged.

Of the visitors, the one who most affected Theodore was Sylvia Townsend Warner. Powys was impressed by her quick and lively wit, her knowledge of French and her tact. It was as if he had never met an intellectual woman before.

Sylvia Townsend Warner was also something of a feminist. The same could not be said of Theodore Powys. In the medieval manner, Eve and Mary are models for most of the women he portrays. A tiresome frieze of white-limbed maidens skips through his books, instinctively tempting the village men and paying dearly for such shameless sexuality. They are raped, bear illegitimate children, commit suicide or are beaten and at best subdued, if not defeated. Their creator sometimes seems to derive a prurient satisfaction from their sufferings: this example comes from *Mark Only*.

Charlie Tulk now sat Emmie down upon his bed and played with her. This sounds very pleasant and childish, and so it was. For Charlie took the rope that was in his shed and, making a noose of the end, placed it around Emmie's neck and pulled it tight. Being a very simple kind of girl, not born in London, Emmie by no means understood this sort of merriment, and as the rope began to hurt her she began to cry. Smiling, because he had brought her to this state, Charlie removed the rope necklace, and considered with pleasure the pretty red mark it had made on so much whiteness. After pinching that same whiteness, Mr Tulk began to amuse himself in another manner that soon brought the girl to a state of meek contrition, so that she even begged that his pranks might continue.

Woman is a compliant victim and therefore to be pitied, but alongside the pity is the suggestion that she herself is to blame for her plight. Powys had read his Nietzsche (in his young days even sporting a 'melancholy moustache' resembling the master's) and like Nietzsche his attitude is one of fascinated fear of a creature of whom neither has had much experience. As Michel Pouillard has noted, in both writers man is to woman merely a means: the end is a child. This makes a thief and a man-eater out of her. In *Unclay,* Powys observes,

19. Sylvia Townsend Warner by Stephen Tomlin.

In the choice of a husband, a girl is guided by a sure instinct - she chooses for the future, her choice is towards a new development. She notices some trait or other about a man that may become an heirloom for her descendants. Though she steals this from a man, she will say that it is hers.

Theodore regarded wedded motherhood as the crown of female lives, and a state of which he was more than a little jealous. In *Genesis*, death in childbirth is said to be the noblest of deaths. 'God the Mother' would be one of Powys's trinity. But bearing children, even when the experience is survived, is a short-lived triumph. The women later grow envious of their own daughters' budding (there is no other word for it) sexuality. As middle-aged women they mainly disappear from the action. And when old they are treated with disgust - though they are useful as a mumbling, gossipy chorus.

Powys acknowledges the force of the sexual urge in both men and women, while fearing it in women. He is a Puritan, but one who knows, who is perhaps shocked by, the strength of his own desires. People who remain virgins, like Miss Pink in *Mockery Gap*, or abstainers, like the Rev. Pattimore from the same book, are presented as foolish. There are few examples of happy married love. In *Innocent Birds* Pim and Annie are happy together, though the union is short-lived, and Pim takes tedious years to realise that it has actually been consummated, despite the evidence of his son, Fred. Fred and Polly are childhood sweethearts and true lovers. Most unusually, Polly doesn't want Fred to give her a baby. This role is taken, and taken to extremes, by Maud Chick, whose long-term aim it is to have a child. Unusually too, most of the couple's courting is initiated by Fred (though his namesake the bull has to be nudged into mating by the cows).

The maidens can be treated with a tender sympathy. They are not responsible for their behaviour, they are like frisky young animals or 'innocent birds', a view shared by Luke Bird, the itinerant preacher, in *Mr Weston's Good Wine*. 'Luke had more than once thought that, while preaching to the creatures, he ought to have included country girls in his assemblage of living souls. Their manner, their games, and all their ways so exactly resembled pretty heifers, scampering fillies, and leaping ewe lambs . . . ' In appearance, the young Violet remained Theodore's ideal of beauty.

Sylvia Townsend Warner was a decidedly different sort of woman, and her arrival made Theodore modify his views a little, if only in theory. In a very early letter to Sylvia in reference to God he wrote, drolly, 'If we talk about Him - or Her as you wish it to be'. In what is surely a tribute to Sylvia in *Mr Weston's Good Wine*, Weston observes that times are changing. Whereas before women knew nothing of his merchandise, now 'it may still be possible to teach some of the younger ones the right and proper use of our good wine'. 'German philosophy' too, comes in for some mild criticism. And in 'A Suet Pudding', a stinging little tale included in the collection *Bottle's Path*, Alice Brine avenges herself on her violent husband by serving up for his dinner a dish made from the strap with which he beats her.

Powys could afford to be generous. The fact that Tomlin, Warner and Garnett all admired his work and made practical comments on it, was a great encouragement to him. It was the first time anyone outside the Powys circle (except for Mrs Stracey) had taken an interest. More encouraging still was the publication in 1923 of the three stories in *The Left Leg*, set in the villages of Madder, Enmore and Little Dodder. By now characters are already appearing who will reappear later - Shepherd Poose, George Pring the road-mender, and

20. Luke Bird. Illustration by George Charlton from *Mr Weston's Good Wine*.

Tinker Jar, the odd God of a figure who comes to the rescue in the title story of *The Left Leg*. These characters often move from village to village. Sometimes this is explained, sometimes not - Mrs Moggs with her chiming bell-like curls and her chaotic post office is stationed in Mockery Gap, where she is drowned, then later resurrected in Norbury and Dodder. Lord Bullman, the usual and distant squire, can be jovial and easy-going as he is in a few of the short stories, or bullyingly unpleasant, as he is in *Unclay*. This can only be deliberate; Powys is not at all a slip-shod writer. He must regard the villages as different aspects of a single place - of Chaldon. Dodder is like 'a wide lake, in which those that lived near fished for evil doings'. In Tadnol, the mildest of the villages, 'the fiery shapes of terror . . . were smoothed and rounded and rendered harmless'.

Characters recur more for what they represent - in Mrs Moggs's case, a nervous and timid inefficiency, in Lord Bullman's his social position as lord of the manor - than because their creator has grown attached to them. There are, though, a few later exceptions, notably again two Tadnol characters, Sexton Truggin and the Rev. Silas Dottery.

Powys is mainly dealing in types, for he is not much interested in motivation. Although he obligingly told his first biographer, R. H. Ward, that the main influence on his work was Freud (and amongst his library he possessed a copy of *Civilisation and its Discontents* of 1930) his characters come from an older mould, that of allegory - not so much medieval as realistic, like Bunyan's in *The Pilgrim's Progress*, a work admired by him. His use of ritual and symbol, which might be called psychological, harks back further than Freud, to Frazer's *The Golden Bough*.

The country people, rendered fatalistic by years of estate life and pared down by poverty, made ideal models for his largely unflattering portraits. (It was perhaps fortunate for neighbourly relations that few of the villagers were amongst his readers.) *The Countryman*, a magazine which from the first unquestioningly regarded Powys as an authentic country voice, wrote that 'the author, the rural reader feels, has lived in a village in decay'. In a later issue it was observed that Powys shows people as they really are, but 'the decent, the strong and the undaunted' have no place in his pages - and neither do complex personalities.

Yet Theodore's view could be milder, as it was in the pair of books written in 1923-4, *Innocent Birds* and (especially) *Mockery Gap*. They are also much more fantastical. Parody by Stella Gibbons and Dylan Thomas (though this did not prevent the latter from some sly borrowing) has left the impression that all his books follow the same pattern:

Minnie Wurzel wants only the vicar; the vicar, the Reverend Nut, wants only the ghost of William Cowper to come into his brown study and read him 'The Task'; the sexton wants worms; worms want the vicar.

Dylan Thomas, 'How to Begin a Story' in *Quite Early One Morning*

In fact Theodore experimented with a variety of forms. *Mockery Gap* is one of the lightest and happiest of his books. Those characters who are unhappy and unfitted for life are given the blessing of death, the estranged vicar and his wife are reunited, the village rake marries one of his lovers. Most encouragingly of all, Mary Gulliver is allowed to give birth to a healthy illegitimate child, survive the experience, and be reconciled with her father. The agent of all this is a fisherman, a sort of pagan angel, with burning hair and charismatic white limbs.

With *Innocent Birds* we are back in the grimmer village of Madder, though the inhabitants have been undergoing some changes. Minnie Cuddy from *The Left Leg* has, we are told, moved to Norfolk, a sad loss to the village. Minnie (to whom a debt is owed by Polly Garter in *Under Milk Wood*) is based on Nelly Trim, not a woman from the village family of that name, but a Chaldon legend. She was a dairymaid 'who, it was said, would yield herself to any wanderer who chanced to come to her lonely dwelling'. But while Minnie is solidly flesh and blood, Nelly is a wistful ghost, at least in Sylvia Townsend Warner's poem about her.

At the opening of *Innocent Birds*, Powys makes plain his attitude towards his characters.

A village is like a stage that retains the same scenery throughout all the acts of the play. The actors come and go, and walk to and fro, with gestures that their passions fair or foul use them to.

Sometimes the human beings who occupy the stage, that is, the farms and village cottages, remain the same - or almost the same - for many years; sometimes they change more quickly.

A country village has a way now and again of clearing out all its inhabitants in one rush, as though it were grown tired of that particular combination of human destinies, and shakes itself free of them as a tree might do of unwelcome leaves.

With that, the author dispatches not only Minnie Cuddy, but several other inhabitants of Madder. A survivor of this purge is Mr Billy, who never passes the age of sixty, whilst his nieces, who serve in the shop, 'remained always at twenty'.

Time behaves differently in a village, Powys explains, with 'slow-moving days and swift-hurrying years'. Days are slow partly because 'In Madder the sun sometimes stands still in the sky for a few moments', curious to see what is happening in the place.

Dramatic techniques these, and in fact Powys had already tried his hand at writing plays, producing *The Wood (The Hawk's Nest)*, *Father Adam* and *Blind Bartimeus* between 1918-20 (and also *The Sin Eater*, for which Stephen Tomlin designed the sets and costumes) and to some extent he treated his fiction as drama. He was particularly good at dialogue, and at handling the local dialect. His touch is light: mercifully he avoids the eccentric authenticities of William Barnes's poems, diphthonged and determinedly Anglo-Saxon. As a result his work is much more accessible, though both these Dorset voices are now largely unheard. (Powys himself, incidentally, could read Barnes's poetry with ease.)

The Biblical language into which Powys naturally fell coincided at points with local usage. Words like 'thee' are freely used, houses are 'a-building', spades 'delve'. Theodore seldom makes use of dialect words, of which Dorset in any case now has conspicuously few, but reproduces instead the syntax and rhythms of local speech, along with the ironic understatement which is a feature of it.

In the early and minor works discussed in this chapter, Powys's world is established as, and remains, the village. The great house is off-stage, as it is in Chaldon. Beyond is the market town of Maidenbridge, and the seaside resort of Weyminster. There is no wider world. Powys's village is a timeless place with few twentieth century references - a munitions factory, a Ford car, tinned salmon. He is not nostalgic, or (as Hardy could be) backward-looking. There is no suggestion, and this is highly unusual in country writings, that the golden age has passed, or that things are worsening inexorably. Powys is accepting of the people and conditions he can portray so savagely (though seldom so savagely as in *Mr Tasker*, which he later described as 'an ugly book').

In this he is very unlike Sylvia Townsend Warner. Her attitudes to the country are laid out in an article which she wrote for *The Countryman* in 1939. Her first experiences were going to stay with her grandparents on the Surrey-Sussex border, where milk straight from the muddy cow made her instantly sick. Her grandmother, who had been shocked to learn the true state of village life, related her findings to the young Sylvia.

One punctual church-goer lived in open incest with his daughter. Rape and brutality accompanied the course of true love, children had the upbringing of little hell-fiends. Worst of all was the indifference of public opinion and the ignorant hopeless animal resignation of the victims.

Warner's later experience confirmed this view, as did her reading of the Hammonds, Cobbett, Crabbe - and *Mr Tasker's Gods*. 'In the spring I went to Dorset, where I met the writer, and read more of his work - in manuscript then. I was much impressed by it, and, further, I believed in it'. It seemed to her then that 'the English Pastoral was a grim and melancholy thing'.

Sylvia saw what Powys had seen, and saw it at first partly through his eyes, but as a socialist (and sometime Communist) there was a period when she felt she could change it. In Chaldon

At first it was the flowers I enjoyed: the wisdom, the good friendships, the traditions, the racy speech, the idiomatic quality of the English country worker - or the other flowers, the *fleurs du mal*, the twists and patiently-wrought vices that develop under thatch, the violent dramas that explode among green pastures. Then my interest turned to the pursuit of more serious cabbages: the average amount of unpaid overtime filched from the labourer . . . the amount of repairs done to the cottages and the amount that should be done . . . the average number of sleepers per bedroom and of rats per sleeper.

This brisk and practical approach is beyond Powys, though criticism of existing conditions is traceable in his work (for example of doctors who dispense cure-all linctures without any regard to the state in which their patients live). Since he has no faith in politics or in institutions, he does not think of change - and human nature, like the flints, cannot change. It should be said, however, that this did not, particularly in earlier years, prevent him from being involved in some practical contributions to village life. In 1910 he set up a reading-room in 'the Coach' (the wooden structure adjoining Beth Car) for the Chaldon men and boys. In 1920, he was for a year a parish councillor (one of his fellow councillors was Mr Diment).

Powys's more flexible response was to the landscape. His knowledge of the country, daily-observed, in all weathers, through every season, even after nightfall, was as close as an animal's. He knew the country 'like an old dog fox'. His daughter Theodora has described his keen eyes, his weather-lore, his knowledge of the stars and planets. In photographs his face is as set and rigid as a blind man's, and indeed he could find his way in the pitch-dark, almost by feel alone.

One November afternoon, Sylvia Townsend Warner was out walking with Theodore. They had been over Chaldon Down towards 'the valley of Mockery Gap'. On their return they were overtaken by nightfall: 'a night when even a cat would have stretched her pupils in vain'. Without hesitation, Theodore picked his way through the brambles and down into Rat's Valley. He knew, wrote Sylvia, every hollow - 'every gap in a hedge, every breach in a wall, every sagging strand in a barbed wire fence'.

This knowledge is not immediately evident in his writing. Glen Cavaliero has observed that the imagery of his work arises out of the described experience; landscape is implied rather than described. His response to it varied according to his mood, and Theodore could disparage it in the same

21. Frontispiece by William Kermode to Warner's short story *A Moral Ending,* 1931.

way as he did his house. It was, he wrote to Sylvia, 'a poor low lived country-side bare and bleached like a worn garment'. The landscape however, was always there, and he was forever conscious of it, though without describing it directly in his writing.

Sylvia Townsend Warner's response was less restrained. She took enthusiastically to Chaldon and to T. F. Powys, and was much influenced by place and person. In early short stories, like 'Over the Hill' in *The Salutation* (1932) the narrator's voice chimes closely with Theodore's.

Like a stone into water death drops a weight into the ground, and the ripples spread. A movement is set up, things are changed —sometimes a life, sometimes the position of an ornament on a chimney-piece. When one old gentleman died at Nice, where his young wife had taken him for his health because she did not like the English winter, another old gentleman in Dorset was moved from the east side of a hill to the west.

This story could have been taken straight from village life (it is obviously set in Chaldon), but increasingly often Sylvia Townsend Warner is dealing in fantasy. Naturally fanciful, she took readily to fantasy as a form, perhaps grasping its possibilities after reading Theodore's work. Most usefully too, she learnt from Powys's economic use of language. Sylvia Townsend Warner used words headily, extravagantly, sometimes whirling into a frothy frivolity. In her poetry, though always more disciplined, she early employs archaisms, poetic inversions, even conceits.

Powys acted as a curb to this elegant, elaborate horseplay. The language of Warner's writings, particularly in the poems, became progressively more pared and telling, producing some very fine work. Her sympathy for the country people enabled her, like Hardy, whom she often echoes, to speak effectively in the traditional voice of folksong. She had been one of the editors of the ten volumes of Tudor Church Music published by Oxford University Press and had an excellent ear, an ear she used sharply when writing poetry (a number of her poems were later set to music).

Some of the first country voices to sound in her poetry are those of an assortment of Theodore's characters, thus taking Powys one stage further. In 'Mrs Summerbee Grown Old', the rector's wife from *The Left Leg*, speaking presumably from her East Anglian retirement, rejoices that the branches of the churchyard elm have been lopped. Freed from its overshadowings, the rector and his wife 'Can walk beneath,/ Untroubled by/ The fear of death'. In her old age Mrs Summerbee can still comfort herself with little consolations. The grasping Farmer Maw, in the poem of that name (in *The Left Leg* he is called Mew), makes an end to his life after taking care to leave his farm in a well-ordered state. His thrifty widow, with earthy practicality, stuffs his coat stiff with straw and uses it to scare away the rooks. The poem, too, is neat and thrifty.

Other characters, invented by Warner, could well have been Theodore's own. 'Peeping Tom', for instance, which is dedicated to T. F. Powys, tells the story of a poor simpleton and his futile attempts to cultivate a barren patch of land spared to him by the rich farmer.

> The plot of ground which the farmer gave
> Did not cost him dear.
> All unfenced and untilled it lay,
> And far away
> From cottage and inland tree;
> Where the rolling down rears up like a great slow wave
> And then falls sheer
> Four hundred feet to the sea.

These are poems which could only have been written after knowing Chaldon and Theodore. Powys returned the compliment, writing the introduction (the only one he ever wrote) to Warner's short story *A Moral Ending*. 'The secret of Sylvia Warner's success', Powys concludes, 'is that she understands exactly how much flavouring to put into a dish - And she never lets the cake burn . . . She knows what she likes . . . Miss Warner prefers a grandfather clock to a gramophone'.

What warms the exchange is mutual affection. And the admiring love felt for Theodore by his family and friends is one of the problems of writing about him. To Sylvia, to Garnett and Tomlin he was 'Theo': admired, loveable, an able provider of quirky anecdotes. Sylvia in fact went so far as to write a series of articles for a never-finished work on Theodore to be entitled *Animae Effigies*. This is a valuable, indeed an irresistible source, but cannot be regarded as absolutely reliable. Beth Car, for example, was built - and probably for a school teacher - in 1874 during the incumbency of Benjamin Hill, and not of his successor, Joseph Staines Cope. Yet a whole section of the *Effigies* hinges on the fact of its being built by Cope. Some of it does not rise above the level of a private joke. In the section published in *A Chatto & Windus Miscellany*, 1928, there is a comic episode in which Theodore, on a trip to Dorchester, agonises over whether to buy gum or glue for his son Dicky to take to Africa. Theodore may not have seen the joke. *Animae Effigies* was never published, though there are enough scattered fragments to make a whole. In 1956, in a letter to Frank Warren, Sylvia Townsend Warner explained,

T. F. Powys was a peculiarly retiring and modest character; and though he assured me and his publishers that he liked very much what he had seen of Animae Effigies, etc., etc., it was still not hard to see that really he would rather hear no more of it. So he heard no more.

The same problem arises with his family. Theodore, sometimes known to his brothers as 'Bob', takes his place in the great family mythology which aroused Louis Wilkinson's exasperated admiration (and envy) and which was much fostered by Llewelyn and John. Theodore tried to detach himself from this enchanted circle, referring to his parents as 'your father' and 'your mother', yet finding his own 'sacrilegious disloyalty' exciting. In his autobiography, John Cowper Powys wrote, 'I am sure it got on Theodore's nerves to feel himself one of a clamorous, boisterous, self-complacent, optimistic crowd'. (He also noted that Theodore wrote, thought and spoke of himself as T. F. Powys, whilst he himself 'was always swaggering and blustering and declaiming as John Cowper Powys!')

Theodore's letters are not very revealing, and so cannot be used as a corrective. He was obsessively reluctant to give himself away and his letters are terse, practical ones. They were, John wrote to Llewelyn, 'like my lectures and your diary. They are a pose'. The whole family had this theatrical quality, an inverted one in Theodore's case. Both 'Theo' and 'Bob' are exaggerations, created by people most of whom were themselves writers, but as they are amongst the ones who knew him best, their accounts are an indispensable part of the portrait.

In any case, Sylvia's love for Chaldon could not be over-emphasised. Her visits brought her joy. 'There has never been a moment at Chaldon', she wrote to Theo in 1931, 'when I have not been brimful of happiness'. She could not imagine life without the village. As early as 1925 she was expressing similar feelings to Theo.

How strange to look back at a time when I knew not you, nor Chaldon . . . and now writer and landscape are both well-known and dear.

Stephen Tomlin expressed similar feelings in a letter postmarked 24.1.23.

I seriously do not suppose I shall ever again be so continuously happy, or tap such a deep well of contentment, as in my Chaldon sojourn; and a very great part of that happiness came from you.

22. Elizabeth Muntz sculpting Theodore's head outside The Studio.

To many of the visitors to Chaldon, Theodore and the village were one and the same thing. In his letters, John refers often to his brother as 'East Chaldon'. His seclusion, his goblin humour, his fatalism, his stony individuality, his passive toleration, were all matched by that of the village. For his family and friends the 'white melancholy head at East Chaldon', as Llewelyn once called it - and as Elizabeth Muntz later carved it in Portland stone - was a monolithic symbol for the place.

23 The finished sculpture in the
Dorset County Museum.

24. *The Sailor's Return,* oil on canvas by Gertrude Powys, c.1935.

CHAPTER THREE

The Sailor's Return

Behold the wealthy merchant that trades in foreign seas,
And brings forth gold and treasure for those that live at ease,
With finest silk and spices, and fruits and dainties too,
That are brought from the far Indies by virtue of the plough.

For they must have bread, biscuit, rice pudding, flour and peas
To feed the jolly sailors as they sail o'er the seas,
Yet ev'ry man that brings them here will own to what is true —
He cannot sail the ocean without the painful plough.

Folk song, 'The Painful Plough'.

Although Chaldon Herring is set in a valley no more than two miles from the sea, it has the feel of an inland village, water-tight, and contained by a ring of rounded hills. Here, the coast is a distant country. Only the emerald grass suggests its presence, soaked so often in sea mist that it glows blue-green as burning driftwood.

Only the grass suggests the sea, except sometimes in the stillness of the night when the wind is coming from the south. Then the sound of the sea can be plainly heard, as if it were just a stone's throw distant. In this valley, sea awareness can sting like salt. Sylvia Townsend Warner felt it one evening on approaching High Chaldon.

It is just here, walking up from the village . . . in a November dusk, and perhaps carrying the afternoon milk, that I am apt to remember the sea, little more than a mile away, but hidden behind the tall downs. And it will suddenly become very real to me: I shall hear the slow speech of the waves locked in a winter calm; a reserved, whispering voice; as though I had come to the edge of the cliff, I shall feel the authentic stab of surprise, almost of terror, with which one realises, as though one were perceiving the true stature of an enemy, how far up the sky is the line of the sea . . .

Leave Chaldon on the landward side and the sea has a few last words. Beneath a swaying sign the village inn veers into view, announcing the imminence of THE SAILOR'S RETURN.

25. The present inn sign.

Surprisingly, for a sea-faring county, there are only three Dorset pubs with this name. One, a harbourside pub in Weymouth, displays its sailor, jaunty and bell-bottomed, bowling along the cobbled quay arm-in-arm with his smiling girl. All is serene and ship-shape. There's a sadder story, however, behind the Chaldon sign. Three brothers once volunteered to join the Navy; only one was accepted. The sign shows the occasion of his return, with parrot and bulging kit-bag, home to his stiff and unresponsive wife. Behind his back is an equally wooden wardrobe, from out of which peeps the woman's lover. The sailor has been deceived.

It's a very Victorian theme, stitched with sentiment - although it does have an unusual aspect. The sailor was generally a saucily triumphal figure (as he is on the Weymouth sign) and more likely to play the deceiver than the deceived. Jack Tar, the common hero, had been a symbol of British greatness from the time of Trafalgar, and was celebrated in all manner of elaborate ways. Jam jars and rolling-pins were crested with ships; sailor-suited children were miniatures of his achievement. Almost any object which could be decorated received a nautical emblem.

Though the influence is Victorian, the Chaldon sign is comparatively recent. Its predecessor was a plain enamel board bearing the inscription *The Sailors Return*. In about 1930, noting the missing apostrophe, Sylvia Townsend Warner offered an ingeniously mundane explanation of the sign, which she claimed should read *The Sailors Return!* The necessary exclamation was omitted because the signwriter ran out of paint (a commodity in short supply at the village shop) and so was unable to finish his work. A boat-load of returning sailors, she argues, would be far more worthy of commemoration than a solitary drinker (even one so obviously in need of drowning his sorrows as the sailor in the story).

It would be a longish walk for the returning sailor(s). The inn lies alongside the Drove, the road which loops past the Five Marys and down into the village, at the furthest reach from the sea. Dating from the late eighteenth or early nineteenth century, the building has thick curving walls of whitewashed cob under dark eyebrows of thatch. Built as it is of the humblest local materials, straw and mud (an increasingly rare survival in domestic architecture), the place has a homely appearance. One and a half storeys high it sits, sturdy yet trim, and moored on the side of a grassy bank. Two tiny cottages have been knocked into one or (more likely, since one of the chimneys is two-thirds of the way along the roof) outhouse and cottage have been merged.

26. The Sailor's Return c.1924.

Protected by a sentry-box porch, the front door leads straight into a short weather-boarded passage with stone-flagged floor and a servery at the end. To the right is the public bar, to the left the saloon, with dining-room beyond. Cabin-like, the bar is crammed with slanting wooden furniture, benches and tables crowding out the floor. A little window obstructs rather than frames the view.

Outside are the fields. From these fields came many of the inn's early and most constant customers: not sailors or even fishermen, but farm labourers, for whom the Sailor's Return was more than just a beer-house. And those sea-green fields held the reason why.

Agricultural depressions recurred with disturbing frequency in the late eighteenth and early nineteenth centuries, especially in the south-western counties. Amongst these, Dorset was one of the worst affected, being almost totally dependent on farming. And the Dorset parish of Chaldon Herring was an out-of-the-way settlement in an agricultural county with acres of its land stretching thinly over the unrewarding cliffs.

The Accounts of the Overseers of the Poor for the village bear patient testimony to the length of its troubles. 'This is the Book of Charity' someone has written in faded flourishes on the cover of the first volume. Inside, for page upon page, year upon year from 1723 to 1836, the brittle brown leaves record the sad doling-out of loaves, sometimes as many as eleven to a family, and other household items, each one separately listed: a piece of calico, or 'a sack of taties for Douten'. The same names keep on recurring - Squibb and Sturmey, 'Mrs Stickley in distress'.

And Joan Boyland. On December 10, 1763 the entry reads, 'Paid for 4 1/2 yds of Blankating for Joan Boyland @ 1/4 a yard'. Later in the same month Joan Boyland is receiving 'a load of Furz Fageots' (as she so often has before). Then on January 10, 1764, the overseers 'Paid for an affidavit and laying out of Joan Boyland', for digging her grave and for a coffin. They must have been well-accustomed to such bills, especially at this time when the problem of the poor was becoming more urgent.

By the 1790s bread accounted for about 60% of a labouring family's weekly bill (compared with 44% thirty years before). Population increases were outpacing food production, and although employment on the land was declining, the number of people dependent on it still continued to grow.

On March 15, 1790, the Chaldon overseers agreed at their meeting 'That the Parish House now Occupied by Richard and Sarah Squibb shall be repaired and enlarged at the Expense of the Parish for a Poor House so as the Expenses in so doing shall not exceed the Sum of Forty pounds'. Evidently inadequate, this measure was short-lived. Almost exactly four years later on March 12, 1794, the vestry announced their new agreement 'to join the several other Parishes in the Expenses to repair or build a Workhouse in the Parish of Winfrith for the employment and better support of the poor'. In a remote parish like Chaldon the burden of the rates would be borne by a few farmers, some of them small ones. This decision would help to share the load.

For a while, that is. After the Napoleonic Wars the poorhouses were full once again, containing amongst their inmates large numbers of demobilised soldiers. At the same time the labourers' wages were falling from around 12/- to 15/- in 1814 down to 9/- or 10/- in 1822. And the farmers were cutting their permanent labour force, relying on casual or temporary workers instead. Increasingly parishes were obliged to subsidise the wages of their labourers.

Then in 1834 came what must have seemed to both sides in their different ways the final solution - the Poor Law Amendment Act. On September 13, 1836, Chaldon and Winfrith were declared part of Wareham and Purbeck Union. Their new workhouse, which had cost £4,560 to build, was eventually opened in January 1838 (after delays caused by the bankruptcy of the builder). All parish poorhouses were ordered to be sold, and the starving, the old, and the orphaned children were carried off to Wareham.

The workhouse cast a long and dreadful shadow, being hated so much that parishes were often reluctant to send their villagers there and instead continued to give them relief in their own homes. The Census Returns for Chaldon Herring of 1851 classify two male residents and five females as paupers. For the others, there was scanty choice of occupation. The great majority of the men, apart from those living in the White Nose coastguard cottages, are described as farm labourers (or, more rarely, farm servants). The rest are farmers, shepherds, a blacksmith. One women, Elizabeth South, is described as a 'Lady'.

The labourers' employment was precarious and at the mercy of the weather; their home conditions offered miserly consolation. The Commission on the Employment of Children, Young Persons and Women in Agriculture, 1867, gives a grim account of neighbouring Winfrith, part of the same estate as Chaldon. Winfrith was, they reported, 'a notoriously low-wage village'. As for the cottages, they were 'Miserable. Most of them belong to one owner, some few being still out on lease. Almost all are wretched. As a rule they have one bedroom and a small landing place at the stairhead. In some cases the flooring is so bad that the water stands in it in rainy weather. The greater number have no privies. They all have gardens'.

The labourers' diet, the Commissioners continued, could only be described as meagre: bread and Dorset cheese (or 'choke-dog') for breakfast with a cup of coffee, 'for dinner a rasher of bacon with vegetables, and coffee again; and for supper probably a rasher of bacon and fried potatoes'. Despite the heavy nature of their labour the people could afford precious little meat. When the butcher's van came on its weekly round they could only buy suet or dripping.

The Commissioners also noted (and deplored) the frequency with which the labourers received part-payment of their wages in cider or beer. In addition there was one cider seller to every 33 agricultural labourers, and the quality of the drink was poor. Yet the labourer was not often drunk, spending on average sixpence a fortnight on beer, with the rest of his wages being used to repay debts - mainly back to the farmer in return for his pig, for the barley with which to feed it, and for butter. He could not even afford to brew his own beer or cider, as had been the custom in earlier centuries. Increases in the price of malt put an end to that practice. Malt duty rose from 9 1/4d a bushel in 1778 to 4/5 3/4 in 1803 - 4, with a tax on hops of 2 1/2d a pound from 1801. As a result the amount of beer brewed at home probably fell by about a half between 1770 and 1820.

So, work-weary and unable to drink at home, the labourer turned from the cramped discomfort of his cottage to the 'warm and well-lighted public houses' which were the despair of the Commissioners.

David Garnett's novel *The Sailor's Return,* 1925, written after visiting the pub, provides a scythe-sharp picture of how life would be there in 1858-9. His hero is William Targett, a sailor freshly returned from America with his parrot, his sea-chest and his black wife and child. The sailor works hard to make his new inn as inviting as any of those condemned by the Commissioners, and a meeting-place for the village men. No expense is spared in making the inn comfortable. As the villagers watch, the brewer's dray arrives, drawn by its 'fat and shiny' horses with their 'slightly tipsy, dancing gait'. The great load of barrels is an inspiriting sight.

A further attraction is the extravagant variety of games which Targett offers his customers. The men have the choice of ringing the bull or parlour quoits, bagatelle or boxing, shove halfpenny, dominoes, darts, draughts or fox and geese.

Throughout the winter such lavish hospitality succeeds in attracting the labourers, and the inn is packed, and reeking of wet leather and corduroy, tobacco and spilt beer:

27. Cover design for the first edition, 1925.

In winter the inn [was] full of men, shaking off the rain from the brims of their sou'westers, or brushing the melting snow from the shoulders of their top-coats, blowing their red noses between thumb and finger, and swigging spirits till their bleary eyes watered again. Only in that way could they face the bitter east wind, the driving sleet and the long tramp home when the day's work was done, splashing through the strings of puddles, and slipping at every step in two inches of mud.

This exclusively masculine world is disrupted by the presence, doubly alien of Targett's wife, Tulip, an African princess. The theme of the novel (as Garnett explains in his collection, *Great Friends*) is racial intolerance. In his first novel, *Lady into Fox*, he describes the effect on a young married couple of a sudden inexplicable change in their lives. In *The Sailor's Return* he explores the effect of exotic change on a small, tightly suspicious community. Most of the people of Maiden Newbarrow, as the village is called, do not emerge with credit from the book, displaying the 'countryman's inarticulate outraged conservatism in the face of what is strange'. So wrote Llewelyn Powys when he reviewed the book for the *New York Herald Tribune* on December 6,1925. Powys was, he felt, on home ground.

The actual setting of the story is, one suspects, no other place than East Chaldon, where a hundred yards back from the village green a tavern stands displaying on a swinging signpost the title of this book. And to any one who knows this most beautiful and most hidden away of all Dorset villages certain passages of The Sailor's Return come to his ears with the actual cawing of the rooks . . . with the actual clattering of the buckets of the old women at the well . . . with the actual tip-tap, tip-tap of the dairy-house knocker, where one goes to fetch his milk each afternoon through summer and winter.

Maiden Newbarrow looks very like Chaldon. And the inn at Maiden Newbarrow is similarly modelled on its namesake.

On either side of the passage was a bar. Behind was a parlour and a passage leading to the kitchen on one side, and to the dining-room on the other.
The kitchen was large and airy, with whitewashed beams. Beyond it there was a washhouse, a pantry, a scullery, and an outhouse leading to the stables.

There is no doubt that Garnett knew the inn well. He must have drunk there whilst visiting Theodore Powys - one of the first of the pilgrims who came to the village for that purpose. Mrs Florence Legg, landlady of the Sailor's Return from 1933 - 60, had a signed copy of the novel presented to her by Garnett along with a shilling to drink his health. Her visitor's book for 1936 contains the signature of several literary lodgers: Ralph and Frances Partridge, Gerald and Gamel Brenan, R. C. Trevelyan and Stephen Tomlin. Amongst the visitors, Garnett was the one who paid the inn its greatest tribute. From his vantage point there, he watched the villagers, putting some of them into his novel, not as they were in the 1920s, but as they might have been in the 1860s. Indirectly too, the novel nods towards Theodore Powys, notably in the treatment of religion in *The Sailor's Return*.

The church of St Nicholas, patron saint of mariners, confronts the inn from the opposite side of the valley. In the novel the church's parson, Adrian Cronk, is equally opposed to what he regards as the unchristian occupants of the inn. Like some of Powys's own clerics, he was 'always happiest when only the eye of God was looking. He had never fancied God laughing at his creatures'. Rev. Cronk earnestly endeavours to instruct the pagan Tulip in the basic tenets of Christianity. He merely succeeds in confusing her. She regards the vicar as a 'black doctor' who, unless she allows her son Sambo to be washed 'as white as snow' at his christening, he will cause to be 'burnt in a fire with devils'.

28. Shope Shodeinde as Tulip and Tom Bell as William Targett in the 1978 Ariel Productions' film of *The Sailor's Return*.

For her part, Tulip pities the villagers, for 'although they could do so much [they] did not know how to live'. Their existence seems to her bovine: plodding daily out to the fields and returning home to chew the cud and sleep.

69

The Sailor's Return is set in a period when the outlook for farmworkers was improving, temporarily at least, as the effects on the labour market of emigration were beginning to make themselves felt. Farmworkers might enjoy an occasional glass of spirits. So it was a time when a village inn could prosper, but only (as Targett discovers) if it had the support not just of the slow-drinking, slow-talking labourers, but also of the farmers and higglers who would use the pub as their market-place. The labourers still could not afford to get drunk.

The Sailor's Return, being a cottage pub in a small village on a large estate, may never have had much of this sort of trade. But it had the support of another, more dubious, yet more exciting one - that of smuggling.

From early medieval times pirates and smugglers had been active along the Dorset coast. Lulworth Cove, some four miles from Chaldon, was a centre for this local industry, an industry not confined to labourers and fishermen alone. In 1716, Humphrey Weld, owner of Lulworth Castle, claimed a hogshead of wine discovered in the Cove. He argued that it was not contraband, but salvage from a wrecked ship. And during 1768-9 in Chaldon Herring, Edward Weld contested these same, ambiguous wreckers rights, which he claimed that his ancestors had held there for 'Time out of Mind'. But now, alas, the village 'which for many years had continued in the Line or Family of the Savages who bo't it of Lord Suffolk in 1649 is sold to a neighbouring Gent. who apprehends that he has the Right of Wreck . . . '

Smuggling was a litigious business, and a lucrative one. It could also be a source of full-time employment for the smugglers as well as for the despised and beleaguered revenue men (and the lawyers). Around 1718, Winfrith had become a 'general receptacle' for snuff, pepper, coffee, cocoa beans and other goods being run from Dorset to a grocery shop at the Sign of the Bell near Charing Cross. Charles Weeks, organiser of this long-distance smuggling run, was said to have involved the whole parish in concealing and moving the contraband. In Lulworth too, a register of 1794 compiled by the chaplain gives 'smuggler' as the occupation of several parishioners.

By as early as 1750, smuggling had grown from a local to a national pursuit and was 'the most conspicuous crime' in England. According to Luke Owen Pike this was due both to high import duties and an unprecedented rise in commerce. In 1755 it was remarked that there was scarcely a port in England or Ireland from which small crafts did not set sail on smuggling expeditions. On their return, laden, the goods were carried across country by well-trodden routes which in Dorset went through the Blackmore Vale or Cranborne Chase. Chaldon, of course, had its share of these routes. Two parallel roads run south to the village: one through Tadnoll and down by the Five Marys, the other via Lord's Barrow to West Chaldon. Both continue as chalk paths up to the cliff, past Chydyok and Wardstone Barrow for the first, through the secretive curves of the West Chaldon coomb for the second. Both are most likely smugglers' paths. In Chaldon, too, the valley road which now curls aimlessly round at West Chaldon only to return, dead-endedly, to the main road, once continued across to Holworth and beyond.

For the goods carried along these paths there were hiding-places everywhere. The Manor House at Chaldon was rumoured to have a false roof - and a recent owner confirmed that this may well have been the case. The sixteenth century stone spiral staircase leading to the attic had been extended in wood for about seven steps, showing that the floor above was definitely lower at some time. (The Manor House also had wreckers' rights to the beach behind the house.)

The cliffs above the village are seamed and herring-boned with paths, the muffled traces of smugglers and sheep. Llewelyn Powys tells how he explored a kind of track down the steep and windy cliff at Middle Bottom with the aid of a rusty smugglers' stake which he found embedded 'like a nail in a white-washed wall'.

All along the coastline the traces linger on. In Chainey Bottom, the Bronze Age valley separating Swyre Head from Bat's Head, there is an ancient, heavy-lidded well. Inside the well, so the fishermen told Llewelyn Powys, can be seen the remains of a false lining, protruding from the sides. Chainey Bottom gets its name from the iron chain which was hung over the cliffs for the smugglers to use. Sylvia Townsend Warner went down to the beach by this chain in 1922, 'an exploit,' she wrote, 'which nothing would induce me to repeat'. Any chance of doing so has now gone - the chain was removed in the Second World War during the latest of the invasion scares.

If the stories are to be believed, the parish is warrened too with secret passages. There is said to be one from the Sailor's Return to the house behind, and another beneath the pair of fields which descend from the inn to the church, where the barrels of brandy could be hidden.

A village church is one of the sites where contraband is concealed in Thomas Hardy's short story, *The Distracted Preacher*, which takes place in nearby Owermoigne ('Nether-Moynton') The list of other possible hideouts

29. The Dorset coast looking east to Durdle Door from Swyre Head.

checked by the highly-determined revenue men include haystacks, chimney-flues, mixens, cinderheaps and scarecrows. Hardy, in his Preface of 1912 to *Wessex Tales*, states that the story is based on true smuggling exploits occurring between 1825—30 and culminating in the trial of the major participants before Baron Bolland. Hardy's grandfather had been a smuggler, so some of the detail probably came from him.

One of the routes the fictional smugglers use is via Lord's Barrow to the village of 'Shaldon' and across 'Shaldon Down' to Lulworth Cove. Shaldon men are involved in the moving of the barrels under cover of the darkness between moon and moon. And in reality the Chaldon men, four labourers, who appear in Dorchester Gaol Registers, Benjamin Stickland, Robert Squibb, William Squibb and Edward Snelling, were all charged around this time. Snelling and William Squibb both admittedly feloniously assaulting customs officers, an offence which they themselves probably regarded as innocuous. Customs officers were seen by the moonshiners as fair game, and were often treated without mercy. They cut poor figures in *The Distracted Preacher* as 'men who take from country traders what they have honestly bought wi' their own money in France'.

In the story practically everyone in the village has a part in the smuggling. (The Methodist preacher is a reluctant participant, the parson turns a blind eye in exchange for a share of the spoils.) Lizzy Newberry, the heroine, tries to explain the villagers' attitude to the doubting preacher.

My father did it, and so did my grandfather, and almost everybody in Nether-Moynton lives by it, and life would be so dull if it wasn't for that, that I should not care to live at all.

Yet by 1830 smuggling was on the decline. As import duties were reduced so was illicit trading, and the indulgent attitude of society towards it gradually altered. According to Roger Guttridge in *Dorset Smugglers*, the death blow was delivered by the 1832 Reform Act, which had a very troubled passing and a divisive effect on local communities. Smuggling slowly ceased to be a national pursuit, instead becoming 'a pathetic and dangerous game for the working classes'. (Wrecking, too, by the 1850s, took the form of stripping existing wrecks rather than enticing vessels to their doom.)

Though the punishments grew stiffer and the rewards fewer, the labourers would continue to smuggle, reluctant to abandon their sport. In Chaldon, memories of moon-shining remain bright. Old trophies - like the grappling irons used for recovering sunken casks - are still preserved, in the same way that soldiers preserve their war mementoes. It's said, in justification and explanation, that the people needed to keep on smuggling (just as they needed to poach) as a means of survival.

The persistence of smuggling could also be regarded as a protest by the agricultural workers against the limitations, the difficulties, of their lives. From time to time there was other, more direct action by the labourers against their conditions, in rick burnings (there were fires in Winfrith in 1844) and the like. The most serious threat to landowner and farmer came with the agricultural riots of 1830, the 'Captain Swing' uprisings.

One of the barns above the village, the long-ruined Old Down Barn, was a meeting-place for the labourers of Chaldon and Winfrith. Llewelyn Powys describes the stirrings of revolt there, and some of the reasons for it, in one of his *Dorset Essays*.

Ever since the Enclosure Acts of the eighteenth century, the agricultural labourers of England have lost their independence. Their small-holdings were then taken from them, together with their arable and grazing rights on the common grounds, their fuel rights, and immemorial gleaning rights. Gone were their milk-white geese, their pigs and Cow Crumbock. In the autumn of 1830 the men of Chaldon Herring, who were then frequenting the Old Barn, joined with the Winfrith workmen in demanding a higher wage.

The chalk walls of the Old Barn were scarred with graffiti, some from as early as 1725, but much of it dating from 1830, and marking the advent of Captain Swing.

During that year the riots had been spreading across the country, reaching Dorset on November 22. They were at their most forceful in the Blackmore Vale to the north of the county, but aroused angry fear in many of the landowners and farmers, regardless of situation. A local landowner and magistrate who showed the most obdurately unyielding response to the labourers' demands was James Frampton, brother of Mary, of Moreton House. It had been an exciting year for the Framptons: first the French royal visitors at Lulworth, then the marriage of James's eldest daughter, and now the uprisings. Frampton, who was opposed to any pay rise whatsoever, daily expected a siege of Moreton House. Militia men were sent in, but no one attacked, and it seems unlikely that anyone ever intended to do so.

On November 29, there was a rising at Winfrith, to which Frampton rode, accompanied by a large body of farmers and special constables. In Mary Frampton's words, 'The mob, urged on from behind hedges, etc., by a number of women and children, advanced rather respectfully, and with their hats in their hands, to demand increase of wages, but would not listen to the request that they would disperse'. The men were described to Mary as 'being in general very fine-looking young men, and particularly well-dressed, as if they had put on their best clothes for the occasion'. Was this out of long-instilled habits of deference, or from an unexpected holiday spirit? It must have taken a lot to goad these ill-fed, deferential people into protest - and the unbending attitude of men like Frampton must have been one of the main causes for their action.

30. The Old Barn on Chaldon Down.

The two sides met on the turnpike road by Winfrith, where the men refused to disperse. Frampton tried to seize one of the leaders but 'he slipped from his captors by leaving his smock-frock in their hands'. As the first crowd was dispersing, a band of men appeared from Lulworth, whom Frampton persuaded to return home. Meanwhile, the Winfrith and Chaldon labourers had reassembled, and began to attack the constables. Three men were arrested and later brought before a special assize in Dorchester (two were acquitted and one sentenced to three months hard labour). A final group, arriving from Osmington, took one look at the solid ranks of constables and promptly retreated.

This modest but unprecedented incident took on an enormous significance for Frampton, and during the next decade he bombarded the Government with news from the Dorset front. When the Tolpuddle Martyrs were brought to trial in 1834, his memories of the Swing disturbances caused him to pursue disproportionately savage sentences for the six men.

31. Bob and Florrie Legg outside The Sailor's Return, c.1935.

These were also years in which public houses were coming under increasing control. By 1867 the Sailor's Return was a recognised house, making its first appearance in Kelly's *Directory* at that date. The landlord, Robert Harris, continued there until at least 1890. Before him, according to the 1861 Census, his father John was 'innkeeper and parish chest' (and in 1862 John's daughter, Edna, married William Ardley of Suffolk - a sailor). In 1895 the name of Frank Hibbs is listed, as it is in 1899. In 1903, the landlord was Joseph Penney. But for most of the first and second decades of the twentieth century Frank Wallis was landlord of the Sailor's Return, where his daughter Florence was born in 1902. In 1925, Florence was to marry Robert William Legg, son of Mary Jane, the longstanding postmistress of Chaldon, and was later to become landlady of the inn herself. Until 1981, when they were bought out by Whitbreads, the brewery owning the pub was Strongs of Romsey. (It is now a free house.)

Francis Powys, younger son of Theodore, could recall the Sailor's Return in the 1920s when it was run by Henry Moxon. The family seemed to have a lot of beautiful children'. He had not forgotten that periodically the pub used to run out of beer. As a boy, he learned to prepare for such dry seasons.

My brother and I would be ready so that when we got wind of the dray arriving we would be among the first to be there armed with jugs and buckets.

Francis's aunt, Katie Powys, is remembered as often coming into the pub after the long rough walk down from the farm where she lived. She also would sometimes bring a jug. On other occasions she would stay all evening, drinking half-pint mugs of beer. Then at closing-time she would leave, her cap slung rakishly over her brows, to tread her way back in the darkness up the hill.

Katie was the sister of Llewelyn and Theodore, and Mrs Legg remembered her well. Having lived in Chaldon all her life (she died in 1985) she was full of stories about the pub. She and her son-in-law Ken Blandamer have described how, in the thirties, the pub would often be full to overflowing, with as many as sixty people crowded around the piano in one smoky room, drinking together and singing.

The three small bedrooms upstairs often welcomed visitors, writers from London and artists, among them many associates of the Bloomsbury Group, en route for Beth Car. Extra callers were boarded out in village cottages. Mrs Legg's mother, Mrs Esther Wallis, provided accommodation for Stephen Tomlin in Apple-Tree Cottage on his early visits. He had been recommended as a lodger by the vicar of Winfrith and without this clerical reference would undoubtedly have been turned away. Like a tramp he looked, in his old jacket and favourite red neckerchief, as Mrs Legg recalled. (Though she talked too of the quality of his voice and his great charm. He could lure the birds off the elm on the village green.) Very few people remained unaffected by this charm. Sylvia Townsend Warner had been in love with him. To John Cowper Powys he was 'a bewitching gipsy-like young William Blake'. The painter Carrington, who accompanied Tomlin on a visit to Theodore, was amused by his impact on the village. 'From every cottage,' she wrote, 'old dames and worthies, children and half witted hobbled out to kiss the hem of Tommy's corduroy trowsers.'

Tomlin liked to drink at the inn, as did the members of the Powys family who lived in and around Chaldon, including, though rarely, the rather distant Gertrude. On his birthday, Llewelyn Powys would send ten shillings to the Leggs, so that the village could celebrate by drinking his health. The inn, and many of the cottages, were opening up, both to the passengers who alighted briefly from the railway and to the colony who settled, sometimes for years, in this remote and seemingly unremarkable place. Stephen Tomlin was rueful about the influx he had inadvertently helped to cause. 'It has been a joy', he wrote to Theodore, ' . . . to hear of Chaldon and its inhabitants . . . It now seems to be the best known village in England. Theo dear, we ought to have kept it a secret. But it would be hard to find a bushel sufficiently large and opaque enough to hide a light like yours'. Gerald Brenan, in a letter to Theodore of 1933, teased that such was the popularity of the village that the Southern Railway had brought out a poster 'marked "visit East Chaldon and POWYS LAND".'

Yet Chaldon was still an impoverished place. In her essay *Love Green* published in 1932, Sylvia Townsend Warner observes the life in a poor village where the thistles encroach upon the downs and thatch is thin. Love Green is Chaldon; the essay is unusually prickly. The roses round the door are showing their thorns.

The opening passages describe an evening of badger baiting at the Love Green inn.

A ring was made and the badger loosed into it. As it turned this way and that from the dogs a kick and a shout stopped its escape, till, fighting sullenly, it met its end.

As well as such delights, the Love Green pub has its notorious regulars: the man who can drink eleven pints at a sitting and the village intellectual who, when 'thoroughly glorious', will recite the Bible by heart, despite complaints at his interruption of the usual tavern talk of 'scandal, bawdry, the weather, and social injustice'.

Billy Lucas, village drunkard, would have fitted both of these roles. In Warner's diary for 1930 she made a note of his appearance: '[he] looked very fine with his broad smooth body under its striped flannel shirt, and his head back, and his hooked nose fitting so well into the swoop of his profile against the window.' He claimed that he would read anything 'historiorical, poetical, scriptural if it be deep'.

When a soldier in the First World War, it is said, Billy escaped the unhappy fate of the rest of his platoon thanks to his detention in a military prison for drunkenness. On one leave, he sent a telegram from the Black Bear at Wareham announcing his imminent arrival. A second one followed from the Rising Sun at East Knighton. Then, some days later, his family received a similar message from the Red Lion at Winfrith. Billy's leave was up before he could reach his home pub, the Sailor's Return.

After leaving the army, Billy Lucas used up his war gratuity on rides in taxis. Beer was in short supply in 1918 and he needed transport to go in search of any pub which might have supplies.

Billy and his wife Betty lived with their two sons in the middle of the row of cottages now called The Well House. When he worked (his wife was the serious wage-earner), he was employed at West Chaldon, making spars and hurdles in the little wood of Clayland Coppice, north of the farm. When he worked, too, he was always on the lookout for half-a-crown's payment in advance.

On his way home from drinking the proceeds, Billy would wade through the river, a safer method of crossing, he believed, than risking the footbridge, from which he might fall. Sometimes he would actually sit in the water. There was a tradition in Chaldon that if you fell in the river you were 'mayor' for the day. Whether a deliberate dousing would qualify a man for the title remains unclear.

The village women were more or less excluded from this title because - except for a few 'of the old school' - when they drank, they drank in their cottages, sending out for beer or whisky, or drinking home-made wine. In her essay, Sylvia Townsend Warner condemns this custom as one likely to increase 'the suspicion and narrow-mindedness which are cankers of village life'. (Not that they would fare much better at the inn. There the companionship is dismissed in the essay as the comradeship of 'a team of cart-horses'.)

Sylvia Townsend Warner had plenty of opportunity to watch the inn, as she lived in 'the late Miss Green's cottage' on the other side of the lane, next door to the Wesleyan mission room and its adjoining house. Miss Green's cottage, 'this small and undesirable residence' as a surveyor's report described it, had one advantage, in a village of tied cottages - that of being freehold.

Sylvia's friend, Jean Starr Untermeyer, stayed at the cottage in the summer of 1934, at first finding it somewhat primitive - and disappointingly unthatched. There was, she saw to her dismay, a narrow kitchen with a solitary, dribbling tap, and a flagged sitting room. A half-flight of stairs led to the two upper rooms. Cooking was done by oil, from a twelve gallon drum, replenished monthly. The grocer's van called once a week; lettuce was to be had from her neighbour, the Sailor's Return. Yet she grew to love Miss Green's, and became accustomed to the resounding clatter of footsteps on the chalk road outside her door, as the late-night revellers went singing homeward.

During the Second World War, in 1944, the cottage was hit by a bomb. Being close to the camps at Bovington and Lulworth, and hard by the Isle of

Portland, Chaldon was the misplaced target for several bombs, one of which fell on the Five Marys, another in the Rat's Valley and another outside Chydyok.

32. Miss Green's Cottage.

'The little snub-nosed squat victorian house' which had been Miss Green's cottage was completely destroyed.

> All in a summer night scattered and gone
> As a dove at a thunder-clap is flown!

By the time Sylvia Townsend Warner was mourning the loss of her house in this poem, she had already moved to Frome Vauchurch. Her tenants, the Pitmans, had a remarkable escape. They were standing in the doorway when the bomb dropped, and were blown out by the blast as the house fell around them. Opposite, in the Sailor's Return, Mrs Legg and her daughter Josie also narrowly escaped the bomb. They normally took shelter over the road when they heard gunfire. But that day Mrs Legg suddenly refused to go across in her carpet slippers and was standing in the doorway, one shoe off and one shoe on, when the cottage fell. The bomb, a two-thousand-pounder, had landed in the field behind the cottage, casting a wave of gleaming subsoil clay over the road and gardens. The pub in those days was fronted by a neat box hedge with apple trees and a well behind. The apple trees were crusted with clay from the blast.

The Sailor's Return survived the bomb - and the war - with its buildings intact. A greater threat was to be posed in the sixties, when the pub slipped slowly into twenty years of decline. Landlords came and went. The literary lodgers had mostly left too. Theodore Powys had retired to Mappowder as war began; Llewelyn died in Switzerland in 1939. By then Sylvia Townsend Warner had moved to Frome Vauchurch, and Stephen Tomlin was dead of septicaemia.

Today the village is quieter, and the shop is a private house. But the inn remains, and under an independent owner has been lovingly enlarged and restored - like many of the cottages in the village. As Chaldon changes, the pub changes with it: sailor and ploughman are forever spliced.

> *If were a blackbird, I'd whistle and sing,*
> *And fly over the vessel my true love sailed in,*
> *And high in the rigging, I'd build me a nest,*
> *And sleep every night on his lily-white breast.*

Song sung for years in The Sailor's Return.

33. Monument to the Rev. Joseph Staines Cope.

CHAPTER FOUR

Church and School

Teach joy. Cast out all modern ways to the Devil. Let the children seek happiness alone. Open each little village school again as a shelter. In fine weather let the children learn in the fields. Teach them, slowly, joyfully, as the grass grows and the trees blossom. Let them learn by thinking, by doing, by seeing. Bring back to them the Blessed Mary, Jesus, Pan, Cybele the Mother of the Gods. Bring back Divine Nature. Raise again the poetry of religion from the ground. Open for the children the best book - God.

T.F. Powys, 'The Rural School'

In Chaldon, it's a shorter step than usual from the cradle to the grave. Chaldon school is wedged into the churchyard's end, its blind northern side overhanging the lane, its southern windows facing towerwards (whether the school is actually in or outside the churchyard was a matter of later dispute). Gravestones, age-freckled with lichen, tilt and slant about its walls. Built in the familiar Victorian-Tudor style of the National (Church of England) schools, with bell-tower and perfunctory gables, it housed the children in a single room of 12 yards by seven yards by 15 feet high. During the thirty-two years for which the school log survives, between thirty to sixty children were taught in this space.

Negotiations for building the school began in 1843 when the vicar, James Cree, who was also rector of Owermoigne, wrote the first of a series of painstaking letters to the National Society for Promoting the Education of the Poor in the Principles of the Established Church, a letter which he hoped would be 'sufficient to call forth [the Society's] sympathy and assistance'. The village had neither daily nor Sunday school, he explained, and little prospect of acquiring one without help as 'the whole of the parish is the property of a gentleman not in communion with the Established Church'. Nor was there a resident gentleman, and the living was worth only £62 a year. Fortunately the villagers had discovered a small plot of ground, waste, belonging to the Vicarage land, lying outside the Church yard'. On this site he proposed to build a Sunday school for 55 boys.

Although claiming to be 'quite unacquainted with the form of application' the Rev. Cree presented an eloquent appeal.

The Society will not, I hope, suffer this little parish, one of the poorest, and hitherto most neglected in the kingdom, to remain any longer, for the want of a few pounds, destitute of any provision for the religious Education of its children.

The vicar was rewarded with a favourable reply, but building was delayed for another two years 'by many difficulties' of which money was presumably one. The estimated cost of building the school was £80. The foundations were to be of stone, the walls too, and 1¹/₂ feet thick. The floor was to be of deal, and the roof, slate. Its usefulness was growing; by the time of their re-application in 1845, the village had decided on a daily school, though 'only a Dame School for very young children'. The reason for the change was that, in addition to the National Society grant, they were also applying for a grant from the Committee of the Council on Education, whose grants were for daily schools only. This they failed to obtain as the Committee finally refused to help them, feeling that they had insufficient proof of the school's long-term viability. So at first the school opened on Sundays alone.

But even that opening was some way ahead. On December 30, 1845, Rev. Cree wrote to the Society (on appropriately black-rimmed notepaper) confessing that he had been 'much deceived in the estimate and now find that the Building before it is completed will cost nearer £100'. 'I suppose', he hinted optimistically, 'it is vain for me to expect any addition to the sum granted by your Society . . . ?' Vain it was; his request was apparently ignored.

By May 5, 1846, the school was still not completed. The vicar had been distracted by the death of 'a dear relative' - hence the notepaper - and the 'continuous rain and dampness of the season' had delayed the builder. In a letter of this date he seeks the Society's patience and another £20.

The bill of James Hartnell the builder, dated simply '1846', shows that he was finally paid £100 although the invoice was for £92. Rev. Cree was obliged to explain this discrepancy in yet another letter to the National Society. 'The man was dissatisfied', he wrote, 'having made a bad contract'. The Surveyor had assured him that the work was done well and cheaply, and the vicar felt that it was 'only *just*' to give him more money. Of the £92, one additional expense was the open timber roof, replacing the originally proposed ceiling. This would be healthier for the children 'and more in character'.

The National Society gave a grant of £30, Charles Porcher of Cliffe near Dorchester contributed £20, and a local subscription raised £33-12-0. Among the contributors were the churchwardens: two local farmers, George Richards of West Chaldon and James Parmiter of Chaldon Herring, along with Mary Frampton who donated 5/- to the fund. The balance was paid by James Cree. A final, extra, £3 paid for the second-hand Arnott's stove, six stone corbels for the roof, the legal fees of the deeds, four forms, two deal tables - and hat-pegs.

34. National School on the northern boundary of the churchyard.

The school had been completed by August 1847, and there the matter rested for a while. Then, on June 30 1858, the vicar wrote again asking the Society for a grant to cover the cost of books and materials. The building was, he observed, being used merely as a Sunday school and was 'useless' all week. Recently 'the liberality of some new Tenant Farmers' had encouraged him to consider opening on a daily basis. The village had already raised '*almost* sufficient to pay the Mistress's salary' (£20 and free lodgings) 'and hope to raise the whole'. The Society granted the school £3.

By at least 1861 the school had become a mixed one. In the census of that year a few girls are described as 'scholars'. Mary Stickley is the schoolmistress. In 1867 she had been succeeded by Miss Sarah Bullen, and in 1874 by Alfred Connop (who reappears as master in 1885). The school history, though, becomes much more vivid after 1876, when the school log begins. This was the year of an important Education Act. Schools were visited annually by inspectors, and the log records the first of rather many unenthusiastic reports.

'At present the instruction is not up to the Standard, especially in Arithmetic but, I have no doubt that, with more and better desks, books and apparatus, I shall be able to give a more favourable report at my second inspection'. As well as a need for 'a proper supply of desks, books, maps and apparatus', plus a gallery for the infants, there should also be 'some accommodation for the children's hats and caps, and the warming of the school must be attended to'.

On the occasion of his next visit, the inspector had only the arithmetic to complain about, but there were other, less easily soluble problems. Despite the granting of a Harvest Holiday in August and early September, the children were often absent in late September and October for potato digging or 'leazing' (gleaning). Come the winter, the children (and sometimes the teachers) succumbed to a variety of illnesses: chicken pox, mumps and measles, cowpox and itch. More seriously, in 1915, an outbreak of scarlet fever closed the school for a week. Children could even be absent for several years through illness. In 1890, for instance, A. Porter was re-admitted after being absent due to illness for two years, while Mary and Matilda Wakeham had been away for 11 months. Even worse was Francis Cleall, who was allowed back after four years of 'suffering with a diseased bone in left leg'. Occasionally a child would die. One death was recorded in 1882 and in 1900 an infant, Elsie Baker, died during the summer holidays.

As well as adversely affecting the pupils' health, bad weather affected school attendances more directly. In November 1886, heavy rains fell and the log notes, 'The children from Fossell and Southdown absent through the streams being impassable'. Snow was another unavoidable obstacle, and on at least one occasion the children from the White Nose coastguard station gave sea fog as an excuse for their non-appearance.

February, a month when the weather might be expected to start improving, brought other hazards. The short-lived teacher of 1890-1, Benjamin Stott, recorded that as the days were lengthening 'home lessons will be partially discontinued'. The children would be needed in the evenings to work on the land. Many were also absent in the early summer for the haymaking. In May 1910 Sidney Lucas was kept 'away from school 9 years of age by Mr Diment'. Mr Diment was the biggest farmer (and a school manager) and he apparently needed Sidney to lead his horses.

At other times the reason was merely truancy. In February 1902 the school received a sharp rebuke on the trivial excuses made for irregular attendance. Sometimes, as in the case of Alice Way in 1892, the reason given for continual absence was 'extreme poverty'. With the girls, though, the problem tended to be a different one. They were more often kept away to look after younger children. A letter preserved within the log contains this urgently simple request: 'Dear Madam, if Possible I should like to have Olive half of the Week as I am never well in myself and Olive is 12 and [a] half and the youngest is two years'.

In 1899 the minimum school leaving age had been raised to twelve, and Olive had only to pass her labour certificate to be allowed to help her mother full-time. Even so, she was luckier than another girl, Lucy Talbot, who in 1907 was reported absent while at the sad task of minding her dead mother's body.

Occasionally, the entire school was closed when the building was being used as a village hall. Every November the Clothing Club held its meeting there; the school was also used for parents' teas, vegetable shows, a choral festival and the Band of Hope. At other times the school was forced to close for unofficial local holidays like the Foresters' Fete at Winfrith or, as in 1903, 'children gone with their parents to Woodbury Hill Fair'.

Most disruptive of all was the up-rooting of families every April. This annual event is described by Hardy in his essay 'The Dorsetshire Labourer'. Hiring took place at Candlemas, the move came two months later. Families aimed to leave their old home between nine and ten in the morning, arriving at their new cottage, their goods piled on a waggon, between one and two in the afternoon. The date given by Hardy for the move is Lady Day (old style), April 6th. It was slightly earlier in Chaldon. The log for April 2, 1912 reads, 'This week is "moving week", there is a considerable migration here, affecting school seriously'. Worse still had been 1902, when the annual migration coincided with 'a very large farm' changing hands. As a result many children left the parish.

With so many and regular upheavals, did anyone learn anything at all? The school curriculum has a resolute ring to it - with subjects like geography, short-division, grammar and needlework, the latter being usually taught by the vicar's wife or daughters. In 1877 singing was taught by one of the four daughters of the vicar, Rev. Benjamin Hill, a subject which could bring in a larger grant. The log for 1883 lists the object lessons given to the Infants in their first weeks at the school.

1st Week Slate. The Horse.
2nd   Flowers. Tea.
3rd   Rain & Clouds. Lines Straight and Curved.
4th   Coffee. The Seasons,
5th   Black Lead Pencil. The Cow.

And so on - but to no avail. Inspection upon inspection brought luke-warm or bad reports. In 1880 $^1/_{10}$th of the grant was deducted 'for faults of instruction'. Teacher followed teacher equally frequently, usually confident that he or she could do better, and announcing changes in the timetable. The teacher from 1885-1890, Alfred Connop, 'deemed it necessary to inflict corporal punishment' on two occasions; such punishments, if the log is to be relied on, were rare.

The school was already receiving some attention from local dignitaries. In 1876 'Mrs Sommerton visited the school and distributed buns to the children'. Lady Bond and Mr Bankes were early callers. But from 1885 until his death in 1902 the most concerned person was the new vicar, Joseph Staines Cope. Thanks to him and to Alfred Connop, the school received its first really good report in 1888. 'For a country school', wrote the inspectors, the results are extremely creditable'.

With Connop's brief successor, Benjamin Stott, the log takes on an aggrieved tone. Leisurely country habits do not please him. On the 20th of April 1891 the school clock is sent to Dorchester for repair (and 'One Gall of Ink 'is received). On April 29, a week after his resignation, Stott notes, 'The school clock has not yet returned'. The same entry recurs on May 11th, but by the 14th at last 'the clock has arrived'. On the next day the still-dissatisfied Stott is complaining that 'A chair which was sent to the Village carpenter some two months ago for repairs has not yet returned'. And on June 1, 'The chair above-mentioned has arrived un-repaired'.

Stott did not bother to work out all of his three months' notice. By June 25th the next teacher, Albert William Mummery, is receiving his supplies - Bacon's Memory Maps, 1 dozen compasses, scale paper, Royal Readers and slate pencils. Gradually the school is becoming better equipped. In the following month, too, the vicar's wife offers a prize for attendance.

When Mummery resigned in December 1892, he was succeeded in rapid succession by four teachers in five years. The first of these, Francis Chartney, was dismissed. He did not take it gracefully.

Received three months notice as the managers are not satisfied with report and say the school is going down, and they must make a change to save it. They are too fond of changes.

(As master, Chartney was hampered by his assistant, Miss House, who was repeatedly recorded as being absent, but who did not finally resign until 1902.)

35. A lesson in progress, from a sketch by Gertrude Powys.

The last of this batch of four teachers was Francis Stott. He again changed the timetable. In 1897 he lists the recitations learnt by the children as 'Selections from Macbeth, The Village Blacksmith [and] The Brook'. His more fanciful scheme in 1899 of using 'A Night with a Wolf' for this purpose was not approved by the inspector, and 'The Voices of Spring' was used instead.

So the log rolls dutifully, dispiritedly on - until 1905 when Florence Cooke took over as mistress. At once the log becomes inkily and energetically detailed, with children emerging as individuals, and often troublesome ones. Mrs Cooke is soon noting that among other classroom disturbances, 'Spitting is prevalent'. By October 16, some three weeks after her arrival, she writes firmly that she has succeeded in getting 'some *real* work done'. To achieve this aim she is not afraid of somehow offending the vicar.

Nove. 10 The Vicar complains of bell.
Dec. 7 Revd. C. H. Richards visited angrily.

Parents too complained when she punished their children for unruly behaviour. She remained unrepentant, but could also be what she obviously regarded as tactful. On July 26, 1907, 'Having received many and general complaints as to Ernest Whitty's personal uncleanliness and offensiveness, I spoke to the boy quietly as to the matter'. His dress, she considered, 'transgressed the most elementary rules of decency'.

Florence Cooke coped with such difficulties as she coped with the bees' nest in the school rafters, the lack of playground and the 'cistern unpleasantness'. Despite regular winter deliveries of coal by Mr Jacobs, the school as well as being 'badly and insufficiently lighted' was also cold.

Jan. 29th 1906 Infants crying from cold. Miss Fry took them round the fire for Scripture.
Oct. 27th 1908 Weather extremely bad, children shivering, teachers also.

The lack of a playground was the other hazardous problem, as the children could hardly be encouraged to play either on the road or amongst the graves. Jim Pitman, who was taught by Mrs Cooke, remembered hasty expeditions to the Five Marys during breaks. Returning from so far away, the children were almost bound to be late.

Yet Mrs Cooke's enthusiasm seems to have swept away all such difficulties. Her particular fondness was for nature study, a subject most previous teachers had perhaps felt unnecessary for country children. Her pupils, she found, responded with great interest when taught about tadpoles. In fact her methods triumphed generally, and in 1913 the school was awarded a very good report. This was about the time that two prominent village figures, Florrie Wallis (who was reported as having measles in 1908) and Georgina Jacobs attended the school. On September 19, 1913, both were absent 'on account of the death of their grandfather - one of the school managers' (Joseph Marsh Jacobs).

The outbreak of war affected the school as it did everything. The older boys were released to help with agricultural work. The records dwindle, as if their writer were preoccupied, and on September 28 1917, Mrs Cooke resigned. Her place was taken by another Florence, Mrs Lister, whose name seemed to spell trouble almost immediately. On November 1, beneath the vicar's report that everything was in 'good order', she has stated in scarlet ink, 'This is not in accordance with fact. The children were in a perfect riot when left for a short time, and on this occasion their dishonesty and unreliability were revealed to me'.

(So, apparently, was their unpunctuality. The teacher demanded that the children follow 'Post Office time the only reliable clock in the village'.)

36. Children's nativity embroidery in the church, designed by Elizabeth Muntz.

On March 4 1918, Florence Cooke makes an unexpectedly sudden re-entry as temporary teacher during the unexplained absence of her successor. Then, ten days later, Mrs Lister bobs up again, to complain on March 27 that the managers 'in order to spite me, endeavoured to deprive the school of the regular Easter Holiday'. She herself is ignoring 'such petty tyranny' and intends to take *'one complete week'*. There has been, she claimed, a 'trumped-up' charge against her, 'to try and get me gone'. (As well as the managers she has clashed too with her assistant, Miss Studley, who was recommended to her by Florence Cooke.)

Mrs Cooke takes charge again until Mrs Lister returns from her unofficial holiday. As if in revenge, and pending an explanation, the managers hold back her salary for two weeks. In addition the vicar and Mr Diment have pointed out that two families, the Lovells and the Lanes, have refused to attend the school since she has been in charge. More intriguingly, they are also demanding that Mrs Lister's husband will have 'the manliness to unreservedly withdraw the charges placed so recklessly against the Rector of Owermoigne' (the Rev. William Rhydderch, also vicar of Chaldon).

Mrs Lister's husband must have been regrettably lacking in that vital quality, for on April 22 Florence Cooke is back once more (along with the Lanes and Lovells) and is noting, calmly, 'Things are in disorder, naturally'.

Naturally. Here the log breaks dramatically off. Its few remaining leaves are blank, at a moment when any student of its records is anxious to read on.

As the rest of the log is inexplicably lost, we are abruptly returned to the scanty pre-1876 level of information, relying on letters and an occasional passing reference. On January 27, 1921, Theodore Powys wrote to his brother John that 'The village has had a very bad time with whooping cough the school has now been closed for nearly 8 weeks. I have never known such an epidemic'. Rowland Miller, born the following year, has memories of the last days of the school when there were eleven pupils, among which he and Sidney Griggs were the only boys. When the school transferred to Winfrith, the West Chaldon children were deemed sufficiently distant to merit a daily taxi. The Chaldon children, much to their disgust, had to walk. In those last days the schoolmistress was listed, in 1923, 1927 and 1930, by Kelly's *Directory* as Mrs Goult.

37. Coronation celebration, 1937. In the foreground left to right: Jack Legg, George House, Frank Wallis, Ralph Langdown, and 'Mackerel' Talbot.

The school closed on September 4th, 1932, after which the building fell into 'irregular use' as a hall. In 1949, the vicar, Rev. Ezra Ramm, was alarmed by rumours of its possible sale. The old school, he argued, was inside the churchyard and therefore 'part and parcel of ecclesiastical property'. If it was to be sold, 'anything might be held there while a service is in progress . . . ' He regarded the prospect of a sale as one more example of the 'Pagan trend of the times'. The Diocesan Education Committee reassured him that they would 'probably be able to come to some arrangement with you as regards future use'. The school is still used as a village hall.

Next door at Beth Car, Theodore Powys most likely had few regrets about the closure of the school. Although almost maternally fond of individual young children, he found them alarming in hordes. During the Great War he wrote a letter to John in which he described his fear of the Germans - and also of 'the tiny children that run to school in the morning. I go into the wet grass to get out of their way'. The reason for this behaviour was to some extent his shame that he was not fighting at the Front. But the children (who must at that time have been under the supervision of Florence Cooke) were a force to be reckoned with.

In his novel *The Sailor's Return*, David Garnett observes this juvenile cruelty. As an exotic outsider, black Tulip is roughly received by the villagers, while their children throw stones at her, and let loose the bull when she goes out walking. In 'Love Green' too, Sylvia Townsend Warner reports on the children who, 'once infancy is outgrown . . . turn to the traditional rural sports of harrying strangers, teasing the half-wit, and tormenting animals. The nature study learned in the school has put a slightly different complexion upon this last sport. But whether the victim be called a stickleback or a "minnie" it meets the same underheel end'.

Although nature study had a more salutary effect than the essay suggests, a casual cruelty towards animals remained an unthinking part of village life. Farming methods institutionalised this cruelty, as Theodore Powys demonstrates in *Mr Tasker's Gods*. 'The cows had their milk pulled from them, their calves taken away; they were fatted in stalls when old and struck down in pools of blood'. Matter-of-factly, the children acquired their parents' attitudes. The R.S.P.C.A. is shown in Powys's novels as powerless at preventing such cruelties, which are of age-old usage. Parents scarcely notice their children's brutality, or vigorously outdo it. In *Mockery Gap*, for instance, a pregnant cat escapes the pestering children only to give birth and have her kittens battered to death by Mrs Pottle on her front pathway. The children in Mockery Gap are the village's 'third estate', an unruly and disreputable bunch who make the life of their lame teacher, Mrs Topple, a continuous misery. Undisciplined, the children run wild, alarming the meek and timid of their world.

The children, though, are here more humorous than inhuman: *Mockery Gap* is a lighter work than its predecessors. Powys was around this time discarding realism in favour of fantasy, a genre not much used in England, but one better suited to the expression of his ideas than realism, which for him then becomes a term of abuse. Miss Pettifer, the ruthlessly genteel occupant of the rectory in *Innocent Birds,* is said by the author to be the only 'real' person in Madder, reality being, according to Powys, generally confined to towns. The population of Folly Down in *Mr Weston's Good Wine* are described as 'entirely unreal' - and most of them are happy in this state. Lacking in imagination as well as reality, they are prepared to accept without question any unearthly visitation for which they have material evidence. The fact that an angel is painted on their inn sign is proof enough for them that such creatures exist.

The people of Folly Down knew well enough that no artist, however gifted, can paint the picture of an angel - or of a devil either, for that matter - without first having seen a vision of one.

Calmly controlled, *Mr Weston's Good Wine* is an assured piece of writing, a distinct advance on Powys's earlier attempts at fantasy, which are often marred by whimsy, as if the malevolent goblin of *Mr Tasker* had suddenly become garden gnome. In *Mockery Gap*, when James Pring is entrusted with the delivery of an important letter, he keeps it for years rather than risk giving it up; Farmer Barfoot in *Innocent Birds* has a club foot called Betty who is his constantly pedestrian oracle. Whimsy, like a sugared cobweb, cloys and obscures *Mockery Gap*, though *Innocent Birds* manages to work its way free. It is a gentle and moving tragedy of two young villagers, Fred and Polly, whose love is as constant, strong and natural as the presence of Madder Hill. A kiss from Fred carries Polly 'into the magic circle of being called Love and Death, that are the two realities of life'. Polly is one of the innocent birds of the title, a young girl who, like Maud Chick before her, is routinely raped ('frightened') by Mr Bugby, landlord of the village inn, The Silent Woman. After this bewildering experience, Polly feels that she can no longer belong to Fred: 'a thin golden cord that bound her being together - with Fred's, of course - had stretched and broken'. Together Polly and Fred walk into the sea and are drowned. God has promised a gift to Madder, and Polly and Fred are the recipients. Death is their gift, and they are buried in a single grave. Mr Bugby, too, is found dead, 'His mouth was twisted into an odd and awful grin, and his dead eyes stared in a horrible manner at the window'. He has been frightened to death by a large black bird.

Innocent Birds prefigures *Mr Weston's Good Wine* in its balancing of the twin forces of love and death. In *Innocent Birds*, death is the lovers' reward, their gift, it is also the punishment for the evil-doer. It is meted out to the just and the unjust alike, by an unseen God whose sign is shown in a fiery cloud on Madder Hill.

Mr Weston's Good Wine completes this vision. If Madder, the village of *Innocent Birds*, is like a stage on which the characters come and go, Folly Down is a place of more permanent possibilities. Mr Weston remarks of it,

From what I have myself seen, and from what you have told me, no place in the round world provides more peace and joy to its inhabitants than this village. A joy, not too excessive, but tempered, eased, and sobered by the necessity of daily labour. With a little of our wine to drink - and that they could surely afford - no human lives ought to be more happy. For a glass of our mildest and least matured should do much to take away the few blemishes of village life, and leave only pure joy.

Ten years before, *Soliloquies of a Hermit* had envisaged 'the awful Majesty of the Creator come into our own Grange mead, and [lying] down amidst a joyous crowd of buttercups and red clover . . .' Mr Weston is this God in human form, walking upon the earth and on the green hill of Folly Down. The date of his advent is November 20, 1923 (about the date, incidentally, of the publication of *Black Bryony*), when at seven o'clock in the evening, time - and the clock in the parlour of the Angel Inn - unexpectedly stops, and eternity begins. Mr Weston comes to the village in the guise of an elderly wine merchant, accompanied by his assistant, an angelic-looking young man named Michael. He has come to sell his good wine (the title is a quote from Jane Austen's *Emma*). Mr Weston is offering a choice of two wines, the dark and the light, which are 'as strong as death and as sweet as love'. Only one person in Folly Down selects the dark wine and he is the rector, Mr Grobe, an 'old friend' of Mr Weston's, who has ceased believing in him after his wife's unnecessary (and tragi-comic) death under the wheels of an express train. One of the village girls, Ada Kiddle, is already recorded in Mr Weston's book as a purchaser of the dark wine. She has drowned herself after being seduced by Martin and John, the two sons of Squire Mumby. In what is perhaps the finest chapter in the book, and one charged with deep emotion, Mr Weston confronts Ada's seducers over her open grave. He avenges her death by frightening Martin and John (a great beast is to be heard stalking the lanes) into penitence, and by sending the village procuress, Mrs Vosper, down into Hell. Ada herself is glimpsed by the sexton up among the starry angels.

38. Illustration by George Charlton for first edition of *Mr Weston's Good Wine*.

At the sight of Ada in her grave, Mr Weston covers his face with his hands 'as if he wept'. Mr Weston is certainly God come down in man's own image. His eyes are grey, his hair is white and woolly, his thighs are plump, a pretty girl is sure to win his approval - he is, in fact, somewhat reminiscent of Theodore. For a few hours on an autumn night, Folly Down has a glimpse of that eternity which, for human beings, can only be glimpsed like 'patches of sunlight seen upon a dull, hot summer's day'. Eternity is ever-elusive, for 'One never knows when one dies, and one never knows when everlasting life is begun'.

The book, unlike Powys's earlier novels, reads as if it was conceived as a whole. The allegory of a village judgement is handled with a pleasingly delicate touch. Mr Weston's visit has been preceded by one from a seller of religious tracts and books. Michael, we are told, has risen 'to high distinction' after quelling a mutiny 'that arose amongst the workers in Mr Weston's bottling department - a mutiny that, had it been successful, would have entirely ruined the wine merchant's vast business, whose ramifications were everywhere'. The allegory is unobtrusively close-fitting and the writing, too, shows a marked development. Sentences are longer and more flowing, chapters pick up from one another, a new confidence infuses the style. It's the work of a happier man, maybe - and the long years of apprenticeship have not been wasted. Powys's best writings tend to be those which employ a ready-made framework, be it parable, fable or short story. Finest of all is his use of the judgement allegory in *Mr Weston's Good Wine*.

Mr Weston is one of the most religiously orthodox of Powys's books, although it is not, of course, completely so. Mr Weston, for example, has never been inside a church as he knows he won't find any wine-drinkers there: churchgoers only sip. And Theodore himself, whilst in Chaldon, saw more of the churchyard than the church. The writer Gerald Brenan noticed that Powys seldom passed a day without visiting the churchyard, where he would 'muse lovingly over the tombstones', and where he carefully chose the spot in which he wished to be buried. When he moved to Mappowder (to the house next to the churchyard there) he went daily to church, but not on Sundays. In Chaldon he read the lesson on Sundays, yet his attention was centred not on lectern, pulpit or altar, but on those who lay buried outside the church. Gerald Brenan discussed the significance of this.

Theodore was afraid of life and deeply pessimistic about it. This set him apart from the rest of that close, mutually admiring clan, for though he was attached to them all and enjoyed their company, he was inclined to be ironical about them. Indeed in his cautious, cat-like way he was ironical about everyone, including God. Only the dead held him in total sympathy and loyalty.

Only the dead. In Powys's more sombre works, death has almost total dominion. It is the theme of many of the stories in *Fables*, a work inspired by

Llewelyn's suggestion that Theodore should write about anything, 'write about that log of wood and that old boot'. It was an inspired idea: Theodore, as he showed in *Soliloquies*, had an empathy with old and battered objects. 'I love an old chair that is worn through to the wood; it is a chair that can tell its own tale . . . ' Twentieth century literary fables usually have animals for characters, Theodore's more often have objects. One fable, 'The Coat and the Crow', features an object very dear to him - and one mentioned previously in *Soliloquies* - an old roller in a field. The coat of the title originally belonged to an undergraduate of St John's College, Cambridge, as Louis Wilkinson recalled. It was then given to Theodore.

The actual coat and waistcoat, after ten years service to Theodore, worked for fifteen years more: for five years to keep the cold from a small-farmer's back, and for ten years to keep the crows from his corn. Hanging as a scare-crow on the top of Chaldon Downs, they were for long a feature of the landscape.

In the fable the coat has come from the same scholarly source, and is hung by the farmer on the roller to scare away the crows. One crow succeeds in outwitting the poor deluded coat, which believes that the roller on which it hangs is the body of God, by persuading it that, by feeding, the birds will be picking sacramental crumbs from the field.

Communion is again brought down to earth in 'Mr Pim and the Holy Crumb' where an overlooked fragment of consecrated wafer is eaten by a church mouse. In this story, village people have little use for the communion service, the sacred mysteries of which they are inclined to take literally.

'Mr Tucker do tell I,' said Pim, addressing himself to Miss Jarrett, 'that the Lord God, the Creator of the world, who be named Christ by drunken folk when pub do close, do change 'Isself into they scrimpy bites of Mr Johnson's bread that thee do take and eat up at church railings.'

Miss Jarrett agrees with Pim in finding this preposterous, while other villagers in any case do not wish for resurrection. John Toole, who undergoes literary resurrection in Powys's stories, wants to stay where he is - in the grave. He talks with his old friend Pim, who is bending considerably over the tombstone.

'If 'ee do happen,' said the muffled voice, 'to get a word wi' thik crumb of bread that be the Lord on High, ask 'E to be kind enough to look over Johnnie Toole at the last day, for I be well content to bide where I be now. There baint no work to do here and all be ease and comfort, and many a merry story do we bones tell together.'

Powys sympathises with this subterranean viewpoint. He once told his sister-in-law, Elizabeth Myers, 'we pass to the elements and then *perish*'. Louis Wilkinson had his own theory about Theodore's beliefs.

Like the old Jews, Theodore believes in God without believing in survival after death. But he does believe in a sort of survival *in* death, and that is why he can say 'He's in this grave', and really mean it. He thinks the dead have some sort of consciousness, and a rather pleasant sort, under the ground. Perhaps rather like the consciousness of plants. He thinks cremation is 'cheating your friends'; he might have added that it is cheating yourself.

There is in *Fables* a surfeit of descriptions of the physical decay which follows burial. One flickeringly surreal tale tells of the conversation between a slow worm and a corpse candle. Here, as elsewhere, there is a joke included about the much-disturbed bones of 'wold Barker' which are never allowed to rest. In 'The Stone and Mr Thomas', too, the skull of the long-dead Thomas (about to be crushed and used as manure) is taken for that of James Barker. If 'Mr Thomas' can be taken once again as a projection of Theodore, then this fable presupposes the disintegration of his own body. Dwelling on these earthy details, of which a countryman would often be reminded, Theodore seems to find comfort, for decay is a natural process and harmless, while the grave is a fine and private, even a cosy, place. In 'The Clout and the Pan' for example, the grave-digger eats his lunch in the grave he has newly dug, 'wishing that his own cottage was half so warm'.

Nature, the source and end of all life, also serves as a consolation to the still-living, and the passing of its beauties will be mourned more intently than the loss of family and friends. In 'The Corpse and the Flea' dying Mr Johnson regrets that,

Neither would he ever again walk to the copse down the green lane and hear the patter of ripe September nuts when the east wind blows. Never again would he carry in from his woodshed the winter logs to gladden his lonely heart by their bright burning of a Christmas Eve. Never more would he enjoy to lie warm in bed of a frosty night when the owl passes under the moon, followed by its shadow.

Mr Johnson let these thoughts go. He smiled a little.

Mr Johnson is finally glad to die. Powys can in fact make death seem a beguiling prospect, as he does in a breath-taking chapter of *Kindness in a Corner* which is set in Tadnol, that most mild of villages. With its larger river, longer bridge, railway crossing and mill (not to mention its resident saint, Susanna) it is the place which looks least like Chaldon. Tadnoll is the name of a hamlet in Chaldon parish and features in Powys's stories from as early as 1915, though with much more prominence later.

The rector of Tadnol is the Rev. Silas Dottery, a good and unworldly man (virtual synonyms in Powys) who exists on comfortable terms with God and with his parishioners: 'Mr Dottery would have been very much surprised had he been told that the people of Tadnol loved him. He had always hoped that he did them no harm . . . ' So when they see that their rector is troubled (by the thought of an enforced visit to the Bishop in Portstown) the villagers decide to go 'and ask of Mr Dottery where the fleas do tickle'. This is an unusually enterprising action for any characters of Powys, but then there's a rare amount of kindness in this cottage corner.

A sadder strain is brought to the harmony by two aged incomers, Mr and Mrs Turtle, driven to the village by their overwhelming fear of death. Dottery tries to assuage this fear by explaining to the couple that eternity is to be found in the grave, but cannot explain what eternity is, and so fails in his consolation. The only person able to help them is Truggin, Dottery's sexton (an important character to Powys), who gives a practical demonstration of the mercies of death. This scene, like so many of Powys's best, occurs in the churchyard, beside an empty open grave. Truggin for his part has no faith whatsoever in resurrection, in fact the idea appals him, 'for no good workman - such as Truggin was, or so learned in the full meaning of his mystery - could put up with, for one moment, such an idea of outrage and spoliation'. 'What sense would there be', Truggin asks, 'in making a poor bone work again? We do know 'twould be easy for God to raise all up, but they two hands of His would be better employed in keeping all down'.

The chapter is compellingly convincing (although the argument might have been more difficult to sustain had Truggin's potential customers been children or young adults). Poor book-bound Dottery is left to see the Turtles to their rapidly approaching end, but it is Truggin who has done the preliminary spadework.

Dottery is the most likeable and most liked of Powys's clerics - and the one most like his creator. Sylvia Townsend Warner, who said of herself that she 'never had any temptation to be a Christian' had an interest in clerics awakened by Theodore. She once considered making a collection of Powysian clergymen, but instead created a memorable one of her own in *Mr Fortune's Maggot*. Mr Fortune's 'maggot' (perverse whim) is to convert the inhabitants of the Pacific island of Fanua to Christianity. In this he is as ineffectual as Theodore Powys's clergymen, though rather more enterprising in his approach.

One vicar in Powys's novels who does try to make a spiritual improvement is Mr Hayhoe of Maids Madder, who rigs up a confessional in his church.

GOAT GREEN

BY T. F. POWYS

THE GOLDEN COCKEREL PRESS

39. Gwenda Morgan's engraving for the first edition, 1937.

Sunday upon Sunday he waits, patiently, but no one comes to confess. At last he receives his only penitent, Tinker Jar, whose crimes are many and awful. He has crucified his son; it is he, too, 'who created every terror in the earth, the rack, the plague, all despair, all torment'. And it is he who casts all men down into the pit so that 'they become nothing'. At the word 'nothing' Mr Hayhoe instantly grants his pardon. " 'Then, in the name of Man,' said Mr Hayhoe boldly, 'I forgive your sin; I pardon and deliver you from all your evil; confirm and strengthen you in all goodness, and bring you to everlasting death.' "

In *The Only Penitent* there is no life after death; God does not give one, and man does not wish for one. The same message, less bleakly stated, is delivered in another novella of this period, *Come and Dine*. This makes persuasive use of the parable of the wedding feast, an occasion spurned by the rich and peopled instead by random guests from the highways.

Mr Dirdoe, clergyman of Child Abbas, invites the villagers to 'a kind of mysterious banquet, that so far he alone had been able to enjoy'. Countrymen, he believes, are capable of accepting miraculous events, as they annually witness similar ones in nature.

Thus those who had often seen a little rough seed of a root, that appeared to have no more life in it than a dry cinder, become in one short summer a great luscious mangold, with wide rich leaves, were not likely to cry out 'Liar!' to Mr Dirdoe for wishing them to see a little wine as a gallon.

The ritual of communion, previously much-mocked, is here joyously and simply justified - though its blessings are of short duration. When they die, the villagers will 'cease to be a separate thing, but become one with the soft sun and the quiet rains'.

The feast takes place on Christmas Eve, and the 'host' is Mr Weston. The food and drink are as might be expected of such a host (and of such an author, for both creator and creation were fond of good wine, if not good food). The village gentry neglect their invitation, being too busy at their own bloated festivities, but the cottagers are all present at the glorious church feast. The story is an affectionately domestic demonstration of an earthly communion, a rare glimpse of the happy possibilities of faith when one is on the 'safe side' of God, though once again without any expectation of eternal life. Powys celebrates the holiest of sacraments without accepting its central belief.

A church can, then, be a merry place, but the churchyard will always be more significant. 'In Good Earth' tells of a man who lives at Doves Hut Farm, a place, like Chydyok, set on the downs above its village where the land is barren and difficult to work, recalling the fields at Flintcomb-Ash farm in which Tess Durbeyfield bleakly laboured. John Gidden wishes for better things. At first he tries to find good earth by applying for the newly-vacant Church Farm, which has the best land in the district. When his application is rejected, he turns instead to the courtship of Nancy Pillar, an attractive young woman with a prosperous father. When Nancy proves as shallow as the land at Doves Hut Farm, John discovers the truly rich earth, which is not as he believed, that of Church Farm, but of the neighbouring acre which houses the church and its yard. The sexton tells him:

'It's a true saying, though there be few that listen to it, that a man be given only one seed to sow, which be himself. He may go out to scatter the fields with corn, but then he sows nothing that is his own. He may take a bride to church, and at night-time enjoy her kindness, but only in common with all flesh will he generate his kind. Only when he comes here does he sow himself in a good earth.'

John Gidden makes the best choice of all: death, and death, predictably enough, becomes the hero of Powys's final novel, *Unclay*. Although this is a mature work, it harks back to the earliest books in its misogyny and pessimism, which in *Unclay* are delivered with a weariness which makes it heavy reading. This is hardly surprising: Powys has said all of this before, if in different words. Immortality is a curse, a woman is like a cabbage, her gods are prosaic, household ones, almost from the moment of her birth she is precociously planning her eventual wedding. Love is once again depicted as the forerunner of Death, 'Love creates and separates; Death destroys and heals'. Death declares that he is the second child of God, but claims all the privileges of the first.

Unclay is an ambitious book; many of its chapters open with passages of philosophical musing or general observations on life. The prose lacks the economy which is one of Powys's greatest strengths. Death at times swings his scythe with an almost Shakespearian ring.

I can promise you that I have never been as bad as those Flemish gravediggers, who were wont to cry 'Welcome, plague!' in the city streets.

Having Death as the central figure was a sound idea, and a logical one, in the progress of Powys's work, but it doesn't altogether succeed, partly because of the collection of ill-assorted mythological characters which clutter him, including (at random) Tinker Jar, Puck, Despair and Mr Weston. Then, too, the reader is bound to resist the idea of Death as a sympathetic human. Portraying God in human form as Mr Weston was a much more successful idea since there is, after all, a precedent for such a metamorphosis.

The use of the character of Death in *Unclay* is the repetition of an idea which has previously worked well. There is nothing new here. The book has a final air; a whole host of earthly characters reappear for a grand finale - Mrs Moggs, Luke Bird, the Clout and the Pan from *Fables*, Mr Balliboy the carrier, Lord Bullman and Mr Hayhoe. Additional characters are re-upholstered old ones, Susie Dawe resembles Mark Only's wife Nellie, James Dawe and Farmer Mere are like James Andrews and Charlie Tulk from the same novel. Susie Dawe, who is loved by both Joe Bridle and John Death, is an unstable character, prepared to marry the brutal Farmer Mere because he is rich, rather than the devoted Joe Bridle, but still desiring Death above all things. As a symbol of love she is an unstable one, undermined by the force of Powys's misogyny.

Susie is not the only woman in love with Death, though she is the first to have her love reciprocated. Death tells Farmer Mere, 'Ah! You think that you alone can make a young maid cry out, but I can do so too, when I come to them. I give them pains for their pennies. Their tortured bodies cry and groan and drip blood because of my sweet embraces'. For Powys, as for the Metaphysical poets, dying also means consummation, love and death come together in a final passion. The imagined death of a young girl excites the author's pen into a morbid eroticism which is as much disturbed as disturbing. And there are, in *Unclay*, other macabre traits. In an episode at the inn, the writer lingers lovingly over his description of what the drinkers will look like as decaying corpses, after death has made his visit to 'unclay' them (the term is a maladroit coining of the author's).

Powys gives the impression of a man wearily longing for death. If death were to be removed, he tells us in the novel, then 'all things will mourn, for the sleep of God will be taken away'. Death is, above all, 'the joy of everlasting sleep'.

At the centre of the book is Madder Hill, its lodestone. The beauty of nature provides strength and consolation and is the inspiration for some fine descriptive passages - but pessimism sours this little world. Powys was well-advised to abandon novel-writing - after *Unclay* he wrote only, and only a few, novellas and short stories, some of which, like 'Come and Dine' and 'The Two Thieves', are still showing interesting developments.

Powys's abandonment of writing was followed by two of the most important events in his life: he lost one child and gained another. His son Dicky was killed while farming in Africa, reportedly by a lion, in 1931. (Worse was to follow as the news slowly came through that he had in fact been murdered.) In 1933 Theodore and Violet, at the latter's instigation, adopted a baby girl whom they christened Theodora Gay Powys. They seem to have been misled about the child's parentage, a subject which caused a temporary estrangement with Sylvia Townsend Warner and Valentine Ackland and also much family trouble after Theodore's death. Violet found care of 'Susie', as she was known, too much for her, and some of the work devolved on Theodore, who proved rather good at it, enjoying as he did the company of small children. His returns from his writing had always been modest but vital, and with declining revenues and the costs of a baby, Theodore once again found himself in severe financial difficulties. As before, he was helped by David Garnett, who managed to obtain for Powys a civil list pension, though it proved a protracted business. Augustus John, told of Theodore's plight by Stephen Tomlin, offered his assistance in securing a pension for a man whose impressive head he had once drawn. John advised enlisting the help of J. M. Barrie, and himself contacted Lady Ottoline Morrell who, as he put it, had visited Theodore years before 'much to his consternation'. On consultation, Ottoline Morrell suggested that Mrs Hardy might help as 'she is very fond of him'. Mrs Hardy in her turn, concluding that the poverty of the family was 'now very deplorable', went to see Barrie, who then wrote to the Prime Minister, Ramsay MacDonald, on Theodore's behalf (John himself spoke personally to the Prime Minister about the matter). Barrie doubted whether these manoeuvrings would be successful, 'as so many people have a strong feeling against the work of the Powys family'. Mrs Hardy passed on this observation to Garnett, adding, rather unfondly, that 'A friend who knows him well tells me that he lives in the way he does because he and his wife like it'. Garnett would have none of this.

They live in the cottage at Chaldon, because they like it, but there is a vast difference between living in a cottage when one is secure of immediate necessities and living in one when one does not know how one is to pay the baker and coal merchant, not to speak of the doctor.

In the end the application was signed by such eminent figures as John, T. E. Lawrence, Virginia Woolf, E. M. Forster, Professor Grierson, Ottoline Morrell, Bertrand Russell, I. A. Richards and Arthur Waley. Garnett, it may be noted, makes no mention of his kindly endeavours in his autobiography.

More secure now, Theodore was never to be rich, or even affluent. The limitations of his lifestyle produced the main strengths and weaknesses of his work. Closing in on what is effectively one small village is a device as spare and economic as his style, and allows him to achieve at times an impressive dramatic intensity, but a village is not the world and to choose to make it so, even when the choice coincides so precisely with the writer's talents, is to make the work - and its appeal - limited. Powys is hardly read today: *Mr Weston's Good Wine* is the only book of his to remain steadily in print, and sadly it seems unlikely that, given his choice of subject, he will ever be revived. Perhaps he would not wish for a revival. His writing has the mark of the self-taught, for it is original, honest, sometimes inconsistent (as a novelist, not a philosopher, he is entitled to be so), sometimes wise. His ideas are his own, and can be puzzling. Death, which he both feared and longed for, is the end of the 'toilsom Journey', it is a reward for the good and a punishment for the wicked. Powys seems not to have believed in hell (his daughter Theodora confirms this) and eternity is something seen in glimpses, if at all. Summing up Powys's attitude to death, Sylvia Townsend Warner wrote to David Garnett,

Theo is more afraid, more tunnelled and worked with fears than any one else I know, even than myself. That is why he is always considering death. He turns to death with relief, for it is so certain, so reliable, so safe . . . he is always afraid except . . . when he is writing (thinking, I should say) about death.

The churchyard thus is central to Powys's work while the church is not. As if aware of its fictional treatment, the actual church in Chaldon backs apologetically into the hill amongst the beeches. Its medieval tower, like that of so many Dorset churches, resembles a lichened segment of landscape, receding rather than rising from its setting. Even its name is not its own: St Nicholas was the name of the vanished church of West Chaldon; East Chaldon church is of unknown dedication. There was a church here at Domesday, held by Bollo the priest, the King's almsman, which later came into the control of Bindon Abbey. The building has, like the majority of its agricultural population, never been richly endowed. In the inventory of church goods of 1552, when Sir John Drayton was 'clerk parson' (the earliest known reference to the name of the priest apart from Robert in 1289) 'the parische of CHALDON HERYNGE' possessed,

Fyrste one chalice with a paten of sylver. One Cope of purple velvet and one of blew silke. One payre of vestmentes of white saten of briges and one payre of blew saten of briges One other payre of colored silke One other payre of rede saye. iiij Aulter clothes, iij Towelles, one crosse of brasse. Two olde surplesses. Thre belles.

A modest collection, even by contemporary standards. The surviving church wardens' accounts reflect the struggle to keep the church fabric decently repaired. The wardens paid out regularly for the carcases of small animals - foxes and hedgehogs, sparrows, stoats and polecats. 'The distemper rageing amongst the black Cattle' was a problem of around 1746. Fifty years later, in 1796, a shilling was paid for a thanksgiving prayer for an 'abundant Harvast' and another the following year for the 'Victory over the Spanish Fleet'. Major bills were often for the roof, which was all too frequently in need of repair, as it seems to have been, for instance, in 1789. Most lavish of expenditures was the Victorian restoration done by Crickmay, whose detailed plans of 1877 show the extent of the changes about to be effected on the building.

Take down the present Chancel and the South Wall of Nave, the East Wall of Nave, the present Pulpit and seats, strip all the roof, take up the paving . . .

40. St Nicholas's church from the south.

It was, as Kelly's *Directory* succinctly put it, 'thoroughly restored', and all evidence of the twelfth century fabric was removed. Fourteenth century work still survives in the north wall of the nave and in several windows, notably the east one, which is an example (rare in Dorset) of intersecting tracery.

During restoration all of the roof was to be re-tiled 'with tiles of a dark red color' apart from the chancel area, which was re-covered in the 'present stone tiles'. A century after this action the roof once again underwent urgent repairs.

One rather eccentric feature of the church is the set of chandeliers, behind which there is a story - one richly embroidered by Sylvia Townsend Warner. While Theodore Powys seems to have shown surprisingly little interest in the real-life incumbents of Chaldon, there was one minister who attracted Miss Warner's amused admiration, and that was Joseph Staines Cope, donor of the chandeliers and vicar of Chaldon from 1885 to 1902. Rev. Cope appears in Warner's essay 'Love Green' as Mr Pagan, a man remembered in the village for his generosity - and for the amount he could drink. Anyway, a man whose custom it was 'to drive through the village in a swift gig, preceded by eight black dogs leashed together in couples' was unlikely to be easily forgotten. The vicar was full, she claims, of a benevolent extravagance: 'In Mr Pagan's days every family received at Christmas beer, a joint of beef, and a plum pudding. Each new-born child was inspected and a half-sovereign wedged into its small grasp . . . ' If such a fulsome tribute was not enough, Miss Warner wrote a hymn to God in praise of the clergyman, in which she interceded for his soul, which had earned heavenly rest through the earthly endeavours she extols in her verses.

> By his merry alms, by the beer out of his barrel
> Comforting, and the confident feet that wore
> The path to his backdoor;
> By his well-met to babes, and shepherdly pride
> To print on a white fleece his master's striping,
> By his plump wiles and piping,
> And the provision of chocolates
> Passed round among the confirmation candidates . . .

With such largesse, it was no wonder that in those days the church was full, including the choir-stalls, while the children paraded the church 'behind the gold cross with a crimson jewel in it'. A man like this could hardly fail to be popular.

Surviving documents give some support to this legend. Mr Cope early assumed the mantle of a country parson. From 1892, for example, he was a member of the Dorset Natural History and Antiquarian Field Club, one of the many institutions disliked by Theodore Powys and satirised in *Mockery Gap*.

As soon as any village or tract of the countryside had yielded up all its ancient history, culled from the gravestones, its grassy terraces, and its silent valleys, to the prying eyes and hammertaps of the grand and learned, then would these fine hunters, with one accord, as eagles to the carcass, crowd into the vicarage dining-room for tea.

(In the summer of 1900, the members actually had the offer of tea at Chaldon Vicarage, but this was declined. Instead, after visiting Poxwell stone circle, they went on to Mrs Baxendale of Moreton House for their refreshment.)

Certainly throughout his incumbency Joseph Staines Cope was a mainstay of the school and a regular visitor. His death was a sad loss to the pupils. In the winter of 1901-2 the log records, 'Feb. 3rd Very poor attendance owing to a fall of snow . . . The Revd. J. Staines Cope, Vicar and Correspondent, died last night. Feb. 7th School closed morning and afternoon for the Funeral'.

And what a funeral it was. Theodore, who did not share Sylvia's enthusiasm for the vicar, later described the event for her in a letter.

There was great excitement. Two or three carriages with pairs of horses attached to each came with grand doctors. And after that was over - all the choir men, choir boys and choir girls stood in rows to do respect to the body of the old rascal! But he was rich or his wife was. Doris will show to you a hole, you can put your arm into it, under his stone, through which Mr Cope creeps out at night to scare the solitary wayfarer.

As well as his tottering monument in the churchyard, Rev. Cope is commemorated by a polished brass plate in the chancel of the church announcing that, 'in addition to many other gifts, he presented to the church

The Organ, Choir Stalls
and the
Electric Light Installation'.

41. One of Joseph Staines Cope's chandeliers in the chancel.

This was perhaps the most lavish of his gifts. Chaldon Herring was one of the first (if not the first) of the Dorset churches to have electric light installed, a fact which much impressed the *Dorset County Chronicle* when they reported the funeral of Rev. Cope. The vicar, they remarked, 'has ever taken the warmest interest in the welfare of his people. The parish is comparatively a poor one, and his deeds of benevolence have been many. During the past few years he has at his own expense presented the church with a new organ chamber and organ, a hot water heating apparatus, and new choir stalls; and his latest gift, an electric light installation for church and vicarage, supplied by Messrs A. & A. Drew of Wareham, was only just completed before his decease'. Unfortunately, the late Mr Cope is outshone in the tribute by his own gifts, dazzlingly described by the newspaper. 'The church was brilliantly illuminated with the electric light, the glow lamps on the altar are designed in the form of candles, and the sanctuary electrolier is exceptionally handsome'.

These illustrious benefits, mystifyingly, were not used again until electricity came to the village in the 1930s. From 1902 onwards the building reverted to oil lamps. Thus church life was for years dimmer without the presence of Joseph Staines Cope.

Just as individual, but more private a monument, is the memorial on the church's north wall to the nine men who lost their lives fighting in the First World War. They included Joe, son of Frank and Esther Wallis, two of the sons of Mary Jane Legg, and Fred House, who was married to Violet Powys's sister, Betty. A fifth casualty was Fred, the brother of Jim Pitman who lived in the village until his death in 1991.

Jim Pitman left school, aged thirteen, on the outbreak of war, allowed to leave early because of the shortage of labourers. He saw his brother and six other men, 'the flower of the village', go off in a waggonette to join the fighting. Not one returned.

Jim was given a job on West Chaldon Farm, and by the age of fifteen was driving a steam engine. Whilst driving one in 1928 he had an accident in which the fly-wheel took off his foot. Ten months in hospital followed and then, fitted with an artificial limb, he went back to work. He became Sylvia Townsend Warner's tenant (and friend) at Miss Green's, and he and his wife were there the night that the bomb fell. Though they both escaped, May Pitman was hit by a piece of falling timber, after which she was never well, and she died of tuberculosis seven years later. Miss Green's, the brick house beside it and the Methodist chapel were all destroyed. It was, perhaps, a merciful end for the chapel, which had failed almost before it began.

Methodism had, in fact, been for a time a most successful cottage industry in Dorset, in places as close to Chaldon as Southdown, a settlement about a mile from the White Nose. The chapel there began in 1814 as a gathering in 'a mud and thatch cottage' rented by John Bagg. Meetings were stopped shortly afterwards as they were forbidden by the farmer who owned the cottage. In 1829 they began again, this time in a house actually belonging to John Bagg (the original cottage was smashed to pieces by the great gale of 1824). A permanent chapel was erected in 1853, a neat wooden structure with a congregation who prided themselves on their missionary meetings. In 1860 the chapel had fifteen members. John S. Simon in his *Methodism in Dorset* has left his impression of the chapel's approach.

No one who has been to Southdown will be in danger of forgetting the locality. Stiles of breakneck construction, gates, brooks, heavy and fagging hills, dangerous cliffs skirted by the narrow path, all these diversify a journey which, with fine sky overhead and dry turf under foot, is delightful: but when the wind groans, the rains plash, and the darkness lowers, is too full of startling adventure to be relished by a man of fluttering heart and delicate nerves. Southdown, when reached, repays the journey. It is a tiny fishing hamlet nestling in a hollow of the coast, guarded by a headland called Whitenose.

As well as Southdown, Winfrith had its chapel where, in 1845, Mr Crawford the Railway Missionary preached to the local congregation and to the navvies he hoped to convert. But in Chaldon the attempt to establish a Methodist cause did not succeed. According to Kelly's *Directory* a 'Wesleyan mission room' was erected there in 1892, during the last and most modest wave of chapel building. On the Ordnance Survey map of 1903 it is already marked as disused.

The Chaldon Trust accounts show that the chapel was in occasional use for some while afterwards. Up to 1908 there are expenses for lighting and cleaning, and in 1912 for oil, glass and candles. Both it and the chapel at East Knighton were replaced by a new chapel in Winfrith village in 1915 and 'permission to sell' was granted in 1921. The building was sold to Mr Goult. Sylvia Townsend Warner and Valentine Ackland later had the use of it and Gertrude Powys stored some of her paintings there. Thus the chapel was no more than a house when the bomb of 1944 brought its short, ill-occasioned life to a close.

As for Theodore Powys, he was not to die - nor to be buried - in Chaldon. He died of cancer in Mappowder, North Dorset, in 1953. A kindly, melancholy man, he was always aware of the darker, crueller side of his nature, and of human nature, which he exposed in his writings. The villagers, his family and friends saw the other, lighter side of him more often than his readers. When death came for him he was, Sylvia Townsend Warner wrote, resolved rather than resigned, but he died at peace, having succeeded in the deceptively simple task of living life as harmlessly as he could. Warner went to see him whilst he was very ill and recorded the visit in her diary.

'We have loved each other for such a long time,' I said. It was then that he awoke, and said 'Yes, my dear. We have loved for a very long time.'

42. Henry Smith, the West Chaldon shepherd.

Theodore had in his life as a farmer sometimes wished to be a shepherd, and two shepherds in Chaldon, the West Chaldon shepherd Henry Smith, and Mr Dove, who worked for Archibald Todd, may have been models for one of his favourite characters, Shepherd Poose. Mr Dove was a good shepherd (though 'a cruel man to his dogs') and lived with his wife in a cottage so tiny that it now serves as a courtyard to the adjoining building. In about 1932, Shepherd Dove, by now a widower, was dismissed by Mr Todd and 'wept to part from his flocks'. He was not to live much longer, as like Grannie Moxon the bee-keeper before him, he developed a growth which was to kill him. In her quiet elegy, 'A Village Death', Sylvia Townsend Warner tells of his final illness. 'Mr Kidd' as Shepherd Dove is called in the story, has a tumour on his face, giving him the appearance of 'those puff-cheeked cherubs which are carved on tombstones'. His swelling festered, and became so evil-smelling that only the warm-hearted inn-keeper's wife is prepared to dress it. The shepherd's continuing presence at the inn adversely affects its trade - and the health of the inn-keeper's wife. The couple move away, the shepherd goes at last to the infirmary, and there he dies.

People in the village, busy with their Christmas, spared a moment to say that he was a good old man who had never harmed anybody, and that it was a mercy he was out of his misery.

112

Church and School

Much mourned, much-noted, Shepherd Dove's was as a real village death.

From *The Nature of the Moment.*

In those far mornings, when the cold winter lay
palely outside and the sky was black,
there came early that lonely herald of day,
the shepherd; walking stiffly back
from hut and field on the upland height
where snow, that cruel winter, hid the ground
and ewes were lambing, forth in the frigid night
bringing frail young ones. And the road would sound
grunting under his tread as the snow packed.
Dark, dark hung the massive sky
and his poor, winking lantern lacked
power to drive off the darkness. He went by
in a frosted gleam for a moment, and that was all.

Up on the hill the darkness was clear as glass
and there was no blur of silence. The lambs calling,
the ewes with narrow feet piercing to grass
under the snow, and the light flakes falling, falling,
made a tune clear to his ear, this old man moving
careful to rhythm of work and music and season.
Down in the village where callous of life and loving
the thatch-rooves huddled, there the winter of reason
bit at his heels, blacked out his vision, and shut
music from ears. The old man past my window
walked, and the steep way to home from hut
was the way from birth to the grave - so slow
he passed, with the dark on his shoulders like a pall.

Valentine Ackland

How strangley fond of life
Poor mortels be. how few
ho see my bead would chan
ge with me. Then searious
Reader tel me which is best
The toilsom Journey or the
Travlers reast.

Epitaph of Sarah Wilcox in Chaldon churchyard,
quoted by Theodore Powys in *Innocent Birds.*

43. Mr and Mrs Cobb at West Chaldon.

CHAPTER FIVE

The Vicarage

At this point the road becomes extremely dark, and here, one on either hand are the Vicarage and the Churchyard, like Sin and Death. Sin is far the worse of the two. Sin is large and gaunt, it is built of pale bricks, it is roofed with sad slate, it has lean Gothic gables and hungry windows, on its forehead is a birthmark like the brand of Cain, and inside it is full of pitchpine and destruction. The people who live too long in it go mad .

Sylvia Townsend Warner, 'East Chaldon and T. F. Powys', *Powys Review 7*

From up on the road by the Five Marys, the house which draws most attention to itself amidst the low-lying scatter of farms and cottages is the Vicarage. The Manor House, the biggest house in the village, stands aloof, while its neighbour, St Nicholas's Church, is overwhelmed by a cluster of beeches. But the Vicarage defies the trees, sending tall chimneys up to meet them, on which the rooks roost, distantly cawing, black and isolated in their huddle.

Loneliness in a village can sometimes take peculiar forms. Llewelyn Powys liked to tell the story of the Winfrith farmer who, whenever he was feeling lonely, would shake hands with himself saying briskly, 'And how do you do, Mr Gould?' A farm could be a lonely place, the cottage closenesses perhaps less so. But the place from which most unhappiness appeared to emanate was the Vicarage - which, as if acting out its own parable, was one of the few houses in the village with any pretensions to luxury. (In 1869 a china closet, office and wine cellar were added to an already imposing building.) The last two resident incumbents had a miserable time there. The Rev. J.W. Barrow took over from Joseph Staines Cope (whose ghost is said to haunt the house) in 1902, resigning a year later. His successor, the Rev. C. H. Richards, lasted on until 1917, shortly before his death. His term of office was broken by frequent absences through illness: the following entries in the Chaldon register of services mark the beginning of his final decline.

Oct. 10, 1915 No service. Summoned unexpectedly to Bourne-mouth, to what proved the deathbed of my wife at Mentone Nursing-Home, Studland Road, [Bournemouth] on Sat. Oct. 9 . . . Oct. 13, Wednesday Today the Funeral of my Wife, Edith Caroline, took place at 3 p.m. The Body was taken from the Vicarage by 6 Bearers, Parishioners. The service was conducted by Revd J. F. Jones, M.A. Rector of Winfrith.

This sudden tragedy apparently unhinged his mind, and the entries in the service book grow scanty and distracted. When at last he thankfully retired there was no immediate replacement for him, as Theodore Powys was to tell his brother John.

Since Mr Richards has died there is no clergyman come. We all found the clergyman a great anxiety, it was really a difficult matter to keep him happy. And last of all he went Mad. That was wise of him to go mad like God.

44. The Old Vicarage.

After the death of poor unhappy Mr Richards, the Vicarage was let out on a yearly basis exclusively, though presumably coincidentally, to ladies, and this seems to have antagonised Theodore. There was one tenant whom he particularly detested (and feared) and lampooned savagely in his fiction. She was an amiable lady called Mrs Ethel Ashburnham. Francis Powys remembers Mrs Ashburnham as a pleasant if somewhat dull person who took care of him and his brother Dicky when their father was ill with whooping cough. Others were more enthusiastic. Valentine Ackland explained her feeling in a letter written after Mrs Ashburnham's death. 'I felt very warm affection for her - She had graces - The rapid bird-like flight of her conversation, jerking from stop to start, like a finch flying; and her quality of innocent wisdom . . . ' Yet Theodore disliked her intensely, both for her respectability and for her renting of the Vicarage, where he obviously suspected she was setting herself up as village gentry. She was also uncomfortably close. In Powys's stories Mrs Ashburnham appears as Miss Pettifer, making the first of her many fictional appearances in *Innocent Birds*, written during 1923-4.

Miss Pettifer comes to the village 'with her green car and her walking-stick' in search of cheap and willing maids, whom she feeds on margarine instead of butter (she is a mean and spiteful employer). Discovering the deepest desires of her servants - Maud's for a baby and Polly's for her lover, Fred - she proceeds to exploit them for her own comfort. She is partly responsible for the downfall of both the girls, for which her punishment is to end up maidless and unable to cope.

Miss Pettifer wore a faded dressing-gown of a faded grey colour, and her hair - at least all that was hers - looked sticky. Miss Pettifer was kneeling before the fire and blowing into it, evidently hoping that the damp paper and the damper sticks would catch alight. Miss Pettifer's feet, clad in slippers of the same colour as her dressing-gown, strayed out behind her most despairingly.

'Miss Pettifer' is a recurrent obsession of Powys's books, and from this distance Theodore's feelings seem out of all proportion to their object. In 1922 he wrote to John, 'Oh God Almighty, perhaps underneath the ground there will be only hedgehogs or else little pieces of crystals such as we used to find at Weymouth - but no Mrs Ashburnham'.

Fortunately, Mrs Ashburnham does not seem to have realised that she was the target of such persistent satire. Some of Theodore's friends, though, feared that she might find out. In 1926, the year which saw the publication of *Innocent Birds*, Sylvia Townsend Warner wrote to Violet:

I have really been rather nervous lest I should hear that Mrs Ashburnham had come over by night and poisoned your doorstep in revenge for Theo's having buttered her front hair.

She was not entirely joking, though Mrs Ashburnham had become a byword among themselves. Theodore literally went to great lengths to avoid her. As she was such a near neighbour, this was difficult. Hence the incident of 'Mrs Ashburnham's Scotties', vividly recounted by David Garnett.

Theo was in the habit of taking a solitary walk every afternoon. Mrs Ashburnham, who felt herself disliked by Violet, sometimes waylaid him and would accompany him with her Scotties scampering about, quite unaware that he preferred to be alone. One afternoon as Theo was returning from a walk, he saw Mrs Ashburnham in the distance, setting out to meet him. Theo slipped through a gap in the hedge into the next field and lay down at full length on his face in the stubble thinking that she would pass by without noticing him. He remained motionless as the Scotties scampered up and sniffed at him, then he heard a footstep, then silence. At last Mrs Asburnham asked brightly: 'Communing with Nature, Mr Powys?' She had been standing beside him for a full minute.

Mrs Ashburnham's Scotties, the black carriage dogs of Joseph Staines Cope, the other black dog that haunted the lane - if people didn't thrive in the Vicarage, then dogs obviously did. And most notorious of all the canine inhabitants were the Great Danes of Miss and Mrs Stevenson.

In 1927 a Miss Choules was at the Vicarage. Then at Easter 1930 Miss Joan Inez Drusilla Stevenson and her mother, Mrs Katherine Stevenson, moved in and began using the house as a home for about four to six mentally handicapped girls. Almost from the start this arrangement disturbed the rest of the village - especially Theodore. By as early as October of the same year he was writing to Llewelyn, who was away in America, 'The woman at the Vicarage Miss Stevenson has four mad girls to do her work out of an institution. One ran away - three times. I fear that Miss Stevenson is a very wicked woman, and her mother is worse' (as old women usually were for Theodore). 'Efforts are being made to do something in the matter - Sylvia Warner is the person for that work'. Despite the atrocities he committed on his female characters, in real life Theodore was much distressed by any sufferings. Some weeks later he is again telling Llewelyn about 'the old woman at the Vicarage'. Her dogs have attacked Doris House (Doris, daughter of Violet's half-sister, Betty, was then living at Beth Car) and so Violet has called the Winfrith policeman, P.C. Wintle. These dogs, the Great Danes, are still remembered in the village. They terrified Mrs Lucas the postwoman, they chased the sheep of the West Chaldon farmer, James Cobb (who as a result threatened to shoot them), and they attacked Sylvia Townsend Warner's pet chow, William.

The name of the girl who ran away was Lily Roberts, and she was, in the terminology of the period, classified as 'mentally deficient'. In other words, she was regarded as being of lower intelligence than the other girls, who were themselves 'of backward mental development'. Lily, who was given 'no time for prayers or devotion', was an Anglo-Catholic, under the care of the Lulworth priest. She apparently ran off after coming down to breakfast in light-coloured stockings and being told to change them. A particularly upsetting aspect of the episode was for Theodore (or so Llewelyn later alleged) Miss Stevenson's 'stupid and unsympathetic attitude towards the child - because of her rosary'. The village doctor, Dr Anderson, encountered Lily as she was escaping. She told him she wanted to reach the police to ask for money to get away. When the police took her back to the Vicarage, Miss Stevenson accused the officer of treating her 'too kindly'. Lily immediately ran away again, and was sent back to her former place of shelter - an institution in Winchester - which refused to take her. So back she was brought to the Vicarage again.

This upset the village. 'The Vicar has let a nice party into the Vicarage now', Billy Lucas was heard to remark. James Cobb, worried by the 'pitiful size' of poor Lily, made his own enquiries, discovering that Miss Stevenson was working for a 'rich philanthropic lady' and that the girls had been sent by various local authorities. This information reassured him; it also convinced him that in the circumstances he was powerless to do anything.

Two people, though, did decide to take action. Sylvia Warner, along with her friend Valentine Ackland, 'came to the Vicarage in a great state of mind, and caused quite a sensation . . . They said the village was seething with indignation about the girl and that there was a serious danger of the villagers coming up and burning down the Vicarage' (or so the *Dorset County Chronicle* later stated). But they fared no better than Mr Cobb, discovering that Miss Stevenson had enough influence to put any child that displeased her 'away for ever'.

What were the qualifications of the Stevensons which gave them such seemingly invincible authority? Katherine Stevenson had for a long time 'for reward' taken in girls for domestic training, sent to her by various county councils, being paid £1 per week per girl. Her daughter Joan was an 'organiser and investigating visitor' for the Dorset Voluntary Association for

Mental Welfare, which undertook work for Dorset County Council, Education Committee and County Mental Hospital, for which she was paid £200 per annum. She evidently regarded herself as well-qualified, and did not take kindly to criticisms from her neighbours.

There the matter might have ended. But then another girl escaped 'by means of a rope from a bedroom'. She walked the ten miles to Weymouth and begged a lift to Wareham, from where the police brought her back. Other girls were heard crying miserably. Mrs Payne, who lived in the adjoining row of cottages, heard crying night and morning. James Cobb had heard the sound as he passed by. Mrs Lucas, whilst braving the dogs (which the Stevensons had undertaken to keep in), was further agitated when one of the girls ran out and pleaded with her to post some letters to her mother (Miss Stevenson immediately forbade her to do this).

The regime seemed to passers-by a harsh one. Walter Miller, the village carpenter, saw girls pumping water, a job which previously a man had been paid to do. They also did heavy gardening work. (Here contradictions inevitably encumber the story. Rumours must have flashed through the village like freak lightning.) The girls were kept in doing housework, yet Elizabeth Muntz, the sculptor who lived in Apple-Tree Cottage, said the interior of the house was dirty as well as gloomy. The girls were officially said to be in need of 'moral supervision'; Miss Stevenson denied that she never allowed them to speak to men. They had 'sexual mania' and were very strong, though for her part Mrs Stevenson complained that only one of them was capable of hard work.

Supervision, moral or otherwise, was after 1932 in the elderly hands of Katherine Stevenson. From March 1933 her daughter did no more than to drive the girls to the railway station when necessary in her car and to conduct the correspondence. For some of the time, Mrs Stevenson was assisted in her duties by Mrs H. K. Way (who also worked for Misses Ackland and Warner). Her charges were, it was said, girls 'with miserable home circumstances, terrible surroundings and perhaps terrible hereditary traits'. Badly treated or no, these girls, for whom life must have mostly been a bewildering and difficult business, were confined in a dismal building in a remote village and were not allowed even to mix with the few people who lived around them. Something had to be done, and in 1934 Llewelyn Powys, now returned, was the person to do it. His youngest brother, William, who was staying at Rat's Barn, told him that he had seen a nervous young girl in a field by the Vicarage and a man watching her with field-glasses.

Full of sympathy for so helpless a victim, Llewelyn impulsively organised a petition which he circulated around the village and which forty-two people signed, including Elizabeth Muntz, Walter Miller, Billy Lucas and his wife, Alice Hewlett, James Cobb, Alyse Gregory, and Theodore, Violet, Katie, Gertrude, William and Llewelyn Powys. The petition was addressed to the vicar, the Rev. Cyril Pugh, in his capacity as landlord of the home. It was handed to him by Llewelyn's eldest sister, Gertrude. Llewelyn, had he been

45. Betty and Billy Lucas on their Golden Wedding day.

121

well enough, would have called himself, which might have made a difference to the outcome. The letter began:

Dear Mr Pugh,

We, the undersigned residents of Chaldon, desire to bring to your notice a matter which has been for some considerable time past a cause of grave anxiety to us, and a trouble to the peace and happiness of the village.

It is our considered opinion that neither Miss Stevenson nor Mrs Stevenson are suitable persons to have the care of mentally deficient girls who, we would suggest, should be treated with sympathy and understanding and not be subjected to too rigid discipline . . .

The letter urged that the matter should be investigated by the Council and that there should be no renewal of the lease pending this investigation. A copy was forwarded to Mr White at Dorset Council Council with a covering note asking him to bring the affair to the Council's attention 'at the earliest possible moment'. (Here Llewelyn had made a mistake: Mr White was the County accountant, but not a member of the Council.) Through Mr White it was published to a number of interested parties - including the members of the Association for Mental Welfare. It was no wonder that Miss Stevenson felt herself threatened.

Llewelyn passed on the news of his action to his friends Sylvia Townsend Warner and Valentine Ackland, who had moved from Miss Green's tiny cottage to Frankfort Manor in Norfolk. 'Another wretched little girl', he wrote, '. . . has spent the day hiding in the hedge like a hare from the hounds'. With the help of his cousin, James Shirley, he has composed what he here rather cosily describes as 'a Round Robin' which he is sending to Mr Pugh and the Council. He urges them to do the same, and they at once complied.

On April 30th the two women wrote to Mr Pugh, stating that they wished to endorse the village petition 'in every particular'. On the same day too, they sent a letter to the Council 'as householders in the village', requesting an enquiry and offering to 'furnish full particulars of all the facts we personally know'.

When the answer came it was a shock. Instead of a reply from either vicar or council, they received a letter from Mesquita & Co., Miss Stevenson's London solicitors, claiming that a 'serious libel' had been made against their clients. It was 'erroneous' to say that the children were actually mentally deficient. The petition and letters were, they alleged, intended to deprive the Stevensons of their home, to drive them from the district, and to 'wreck' Miss Stevenson's career. A full apology was demanded.

At first it seemed as if their demands might be met. Valentine Ackland wrote to Llewelyn in reference to the solicitor's letter, observing that

Mesquita were trying to rush them. She and Sylvia had no desire to apologise, she emphasised, but 'money IS SHORT'.

Money was the problem. A moral stand, as they saw it, could prove expensive. Valentine then wrote to Llewelyn's wife, Alyse Gregory, about the bad news that their last hope, the Winfrith policeman P.C. Wintle, was 'not able to help at all'. She feared the Stevensons would win a libel case. What they should do, Miss Ackland suggested, was to apologise, but insist upon the apology being published in the newspapers, thereby indirectly incriminating the Vicarage ladies. A few days later in May she wrote again to Llewelyn, stressing that they wanted to apologise and acknowledging that he might regard this as desertion. In this approach she was supported by her friend, who also wrote advocating apology, preferring 'damages to our pride rather than damages in her paw' - and expressing regret in her turn for these 'passionately sordid sentiments'.

Llewelyn's brother Albert advocated a cautious approach too. In an undated letter to Theodore he suggested that they should explain that they were anxious about conditions in the home, and so were motivated by disinterested concern for the public good, but were prepared to apologise for 'any excess' in their demands.

The impression given by the extant papers is that Llewelyn would have preferred to hold firm. However, under pressure, a letter was drafted by way of apology in which the three said that they 'did not intend to suggest that Miss Stevenson was inexperienced in her professional work as an organiser' but that in her work at the Vicarage both she and her mother lacked 'generous understanding', consideration and sympathy. 'We are under the impression,' they said, 'that Miss Stevenson's admirable magisterial qualities might be used in a more appropriate sphere'. They would have liked the opportunity to explain themselves to the local authorities. Instead, and unfairly, they had been threatened by Miss Stevenson's London lawyer.

Probably due to Llewelyn's reluctance, this apology was slow in appearing. On June 8, Warner and Ackland's (also London-based) lawyers, Ellis Peirs, demanded its delivery. 'Miss Stevenson', they announced, 'is in danger of losing her employment' and the Vicarage had been inspected by the Ministry of Health.

They were to be disappointed. The petitioners refused to sign because of the concluding paragraph of the document which had been prepared for them. This read: 'It is understood that should Mrs or Miss Stevenson ultimately sustain any loss or damage as a consequence of these statements it will be made good to them notwithstanding this Apology'. In a letter to the Stevensons' lawyers the petitioners said that they had so far been conciliatory but would now welcome an enquiry, and were prepared to take legal action. (They also pointed out that their initial letter had been passed as unlibellous.)

In the midst of this delicately-worded dispute, the original claims of the Chaldon villagers were being justified. On May 11 the Vicarage home was inspected by Dr Douglas Turner, a representative of the N.S.P.C.C., in response to the complaints. Dr Turner found among the inmates some borderline cases (as he put it) and one 'feeble-minded' girl, and he called upon Mrs Stevenson to notify the board of her reception of this girl. After his action, he assumed, Mrs Stevenson 'will be very much under official surveillance'.

This did not mean, however, the end of the case. If money was to be paid to the Stevensons as part of the apology, then there was nothing to be lost by persisting with the allegations. The defendants refused to sign, and so Mesquita issued a writ of libel against Llewelyn, Misses Ackland and Warner - and James Cobb, the West Chaldon farmer, who, despite Llewelyn's efforts to dissuade him, instructed his Dorchester solicitor, Symonds, for whom Ellis Peirs were the London agent, to enter an appearance on his behalf (and, if need be, for Mr and Mrs T. F. Powys as well).

The affair was now serious, not least because of the state of Llewelyn's health. He suffered from tuberculosis, complicated by a stomach ulcer, and in 1933 had almost died, making a slow and intermittent recovery through 1934. His brother John, who was staying at Rat's Barn for six months of that year (and who was, by a strange coincidence, unwillingly involved in a libel case of his own over his novel *A Glastonbury Romance*), lent his support to his brother, reading to him daily and otherwise helping Alyse. Whilst at Rat's Barn he made a 'rough tentative beginning' to a work which was to become *Maiden Castle*. Hugh Marriott Dodington, who had moved into the Manor House, was also indignantly sympathetic and, Llewelyn wrote to Sylvia Townsend Warner, came up to see me, driving behind his two little asses'.

The worry of the case was obviously an additional strain on Llewelyn's already poor physical state. But he persevered. It is difficult to be certain about the chronology of events in the following few months as those papers that remain, written in flurry or fury, are disordered and largely undated. When Ellis Peirs asked to see all the letters passing between Chaldon and Frankfort Manor, Sloley, some of them were destroyed. A code was drawn up by the three correspondents for future use, but does not seem to have been employed.

Mesquita & Co. gave vent to a good deal of legal hysteria on discovering that no apology was forthcoming. They took this to mean that Llewelyn and his friends were suggesting that 'each of the Plaintiffs was of such bad character and conduct and such an undesirable, unscrupulous and turbulent member of the community' that she ought to be expelled - and that Miss Stevenson's 'harshness and incompetence' made her wholly unfitted for her work.

46. John Cowper Powys, Violet Powys and T F Powys at Beth Car.

Becoming somewhat alarmed at the turn events were taking, Llewelyn and Alyse consulted Lady Frances Warwick for help. She had read Llewelyn's essay 'A House of Correction' when it was published in *Country Life* in 1932. This described the sufferings of a sheepdog, and provoked a heartfelt response from much of its audience, Lady Warwick included. Soon she was reading more of Llewelyn's work, and in 1934 visited him at Chydyok, his home on Chaldon Down. Lady Warwick was interested in child welfare and wrote on Llewelyn's behalf to the N.S.P.C.C. only to discover that the home had already been inspected by them, and that they believed that the case would be withdrawn. In her letters Lady Warwick seems confident that this will happen, or that the case will be delayed - or that the defendants will win. With hindsight her attitude is understandable, but unrealistic.

Meanwhile, Miss Stevenson was pressing for the case to be heard in London, where she would be sure to avoid 'local prejudice'. Ellis advised Llewelyn to make a stand against such a move. Transporting witnesses would be expensive, and a Special Jury in London would, in the event of their losing the case, award much heavier damages than its Dorchester equivalent.

Despite Lady Warwick, Llewelyn went on preparing for a possible court case. He was concerned about witnesses: some of the villagers who had seemed prepared to give evidence later denied noticing anything. There was also the disappointment over P.C. Wintle. Llewelyn tried to trace a Miss Boudy, one-time assistant matron of the home now in Bath or Bristol, whom he suspected of being unfairly dismissed by the Stevensons, but this plan came to nothing. He was reassured by the support of James Cobb, whom he described as 'the John Bunyan of Chaldon', an honest and unhypocritical man. Mrs Lucas too, postwoman and household help at Chydyok, had remained steady. She was, Llewelyn wrote, in her simple goodness, 'a perfect type of Dorset village woman'. (This was not how his sister Gertrude described her on the occasions when she failed to turn up for the cleaning.)

Llewelyn's defence, as drafted in his papers, was a straightforward, honourable one.

We heard of the children crying in the night. They were heard again by people passing. We never heard of happiness . . . In my innocence I thought that if I got up a petition of enquiry [something would be done]. It never seemed possible . . . I would be leading simple people into the law courts.

The County Council had not investigated, while the Welfare Committee hadn't even bothered to reply. He felt that old Mrs Stevenson was unfit to look after 'such unfortunate children'. As for Miss Stevenson, who was anyway absent five days a week, she was 'a capable women but a hard one'. The Stevensons had got into the Vicarage 'by a sly reticence about their intentions and under the first inspection they were found with a child who should never have been there'. He concluded that the home was 'one of the worst pockets of human woe in the county'.

January 17, 1935, was the date finally fixed for the trial. Up to the last moment there was some doubt as to whether Llewelyn would be well enough

126

to attend. He was determined to go. 'Nothing will dissuade him from going', Alyse wrote despairingly in her journal. Betty Muntz offered him the use of her sofa bed in Apple-Tree Cottage to rest on after the long rough journey down from Chydyok. Florence Hardy, widow of Thomas, who had herself made enquiries about the home, offered him the use of her car. Llewelyn wrote,

47. Llewelyn Powys arriving at court in Dorchester, 1935.

I have set my heart on getting in if I can and am to be carried over the downs in an armchair placed in a dog cart like some buggerly Buddha for the populace to bawl after and the seagulls to molest - a 'proper guy' - swaying this way and that above the heads of all. On the village green I am to be met by Mrs Thomas Hardy's car and conveyed to the Antelope where John has bespoken a room - no. 18 - and will be waiting for me. The next day, all being well, I shall appear in court . . . if I see real undiluted blood I shall turn tail wherever I am. For four days I have had discoloration and even a little this morning, but never enough for me to be certain that I could not make the triumphal entry into Dorchester and 'get away with it'.

Despite the fact that the N.S.P.C.C., and afterward the Ministry of Health, had inspected the home, neither of their inspections could be used as evidence as the matter was already sub judice when action was taken. The case hinged on whether or not the defendants had acted with malice when they published the letters. (If Llewelyn had written 'Private and Personal' on the petition to Mr Pugh and Mr White, then the 'Occasion of Publication' would have been privileged and the possibility of being sued for libel

127

minimal. As it was, the judge, Mr Justice Finlay, ruled that there was 'qualified' privilege.) The plaintiffs' council tried to prove that the Stevensons had offended the Powyses by failing to return a call when they first came to the village. According to Llewelyn, he had only ever encountered Miss Stevenson twice whilst out walking (and had admired her Great Dane). He had never met Mrs Stevenson at all.

The judge directed the jury that the only question they must decide was whether or not the defendants had acted with malice. After ninety minutes the jury returned and announced that they found malice against all four defendants. They awarded Mrs Stevenson £100 and Miss Stevenson damages of £75, of which £120 was to be paid by Messrs Powys and Cobb (with Mr Powys alone paying an extra £5), Miss Warner and Miss Ackland together paying £50. Thus was justice done.

The case caused a stir, and not just a local one. The court was packed with county dignitaries, and the proceedings were reported at length in the *Dorset County Chronicle*. Reports also appeared in The *Times* and The *News of the World* where the front page for Sunday January 20 read 'DYING AUTHOR IN COURT DRAMA'. 'Evidence in a Whisper', declared The *People*.

One odd outcome of this dubious celebrity was that Llewelyn was invited by another Sunday newspaper to write an article on the 'Meditations of a Dying Man'. 'At night a motor came up here we thought it was about the case but it was a Sunday newspaper getting Lulu to write an essay', Gertrude recorded. The paper seems to have been somewhat disconcerted by the article it received, which was profoundly philosophical.

We are shadows, one of a myriad ephemeral beings that have come mysteriously to knowledge on a rainbow planet that is tumbling through a physical universe of inconceivable dimensions . . .

The newspaper proposed that he should rewrite the article as it had 'rather flown over the heads of the average reader' [sic] with its 'excursions into philosophy etc.' This Llewelyn declined to do. He had, though, benefited in one way from the experience - his health had temporarily improved. Sylvia Townsend Warner noted in a letter written immediately after the trial. 'As for Llewelyn, he is getting better daily. His kill or cure jaunt did him most decisive good'.

Llewelyn received many letters of support and sympathy, amongst them several from the American poetess Edna St Vincent Millay who had visited him at Chydyok, offering him financial help. When Llewelyn and Alyse refused to take it, she replied,

I know what it, is of course. It is that dingy law-suit and the Two-Hundred-Pound-Look of Mrs Nincom and her daughter that have made you two clear beings think about money in this smudgy way. You must both send your wings to the cleaner.

Although he refused St Vincent Millay, Llewelyn did allow other friends to pay the lawyers' bills. Amongst them was Rivers Pollock, a magistrate and contemporary of Llewelyn's at Cambridge who had given advice throughout, and was appalled by the outcome of the case. Losing the case, Llewelyn still achieved his aim: the home had been inspected, but it had been a costly procedure. The Stevensons did not stay much longer at the Vicarage, life there must have been uncomfortable for them. By July 23, 1937, Theodore was writing to Llewelyn that the house was now empty 'and may it remain so'. Valentine Ackland and Sylvia Townsend Warner took a look around the empty building. 'It smelt of old roast-meat and of dirt', Valentine wrote. 'The servant's bedroom is tiny and filthy and has an old iron bed in it with a flock mattress of about two-inches thick . . . The ceilings are stained with damp. It is a *vile* house'.

On the same unforgiving note Llewelyn wrote to James Cobb, 'that monstrous dragon and her Dam have been conducted by the devil their father out of our happy valley'.

Llewelyn continued to regard James Cobb as the hero of the episode, the man whom he believed alone stood 'solid as a rock' and who insisted on paying his own fine. Powys's *The Twelve Months* (1936) is dedicated 'To my friend and neighbour James Cobb of West Chaldon'. And one of Robert Gibbing's superb engravings for the book is of the medieval-seeming barns of Cobb's farm, square under their unexpected cliff.

48. West Chaldon barns by Robert Gibbings.

49. Granny Moxon photographed by Valentine Ackland.

CHAPTER SIX

Rat's Barn

'To Theodore Francis Powys'

I am made happy,
For now I can vouch
When I lie cold
That others will live to love
The old oak posts
The flocks and birds
That thrive and dwell
On Chaldon Heights.

Katie Powys

Rat's Barn is difficult to find. It sits on the curve of a hidden valley with great barn, courtyard and stockman's cottage, self-contained and inward-turning, half-haunted. The stone barn has doors at each end high enough for a hay waggon's entry but they have gone now, as has the roof. The courtyard is choked with elder and brambles.

The cottage too is deserted, its tiled roof slowly dropping in, neglected and forlorn as a dead elm. The place is empty now except for the rabbits, hares, foxes, owls - and rats. Rat's Barn is the local name for it; officially it is still 34 West Chaldon, the number once clearly marked upon the door by a round enamel plaque. Amongst the neighbouring fields are Rat's House and Mount Misery.

A late eighteenth century building, Rat's Barn has been deserted before in its history, though within living memory a family of carters, the Whittys, were occupying the place. The cottage was in need of repair when William

Powys, youngest of the brothers rented it as a holiday home for himself and his family when they came on visits from their farm in Kenya. In those days, as now, it was according to Alyse Gregory, 'totally isolated, to be reached only by climbing up and down steep gorse strewn slopes and traversing wide flinty fields enclosed by barbed wire'. One of William's sisters, Catharine Edith Philippa (usually known as Katie), very often made that journey. She would spend the night there, in all weathers, having lit a fire in the huge and blackened fireplace. Awakening at dawn, she would walk up to the sea and return along the cliff to where she lived at Chydyok.

50. Rat's Barn.

Adjoining Chydyok Farm is the field known as Tumbledown (or Stumbledown) about which Katie wrote more than one of her poems. In its vast curving space she felt she could freely become as a 'gorsebush,/ or a storm-bent thorn,/ which separate stands/ Against a distant fence'. When this stretch of ancient downland was ploughed for the first time in recent years - if not the first time ever - Katie was bitterly upset, and in a poem entitled 'A Hateful Day' bemoaned the loss of her refuge. It was an almost physical blow to someone who identified as much as Katie did with the landscape of folded downland - and of sea.

Beside that same sea, but in Devon, occurred the most enduring experience of her life. As a girl, Katie took holidays at Sidmouth with her father, Charles, whose favourite daughter she was, and with her youngest sister, Lucy, to whom she was also particularly close. Whilst on the second of these holidays, Katie came to know the fishermen brothers Bob and Tom Woolley, who would sometimes take trippers out in their boat. Through them she met Bob Woolley's lodger from 1906, Stephen Reynolds.

An affluent and lonely young man, educated at Manchester University, Reynolds came to regard the rough-and-ready (though well-fed) Woolley household as his adopted family, the crowded cottage as his only home. He went out fishing with the brothers, eventually becoming an accepted authority on fishing methods (which led to his later appointment as Resident Inspector of Fisheries for the south-western area). In 1908 his record of life with the Woolleys, *A Poor Man's House*, was published, the first of his books and the single success. Reynolds was grateful to the Woolleys for the warmth of their welcome and for their considered acceptance of him. In his books he is able to describe at first hand the harsh, independent life of the fishermen, ever at the mercy of the unpredictable sea. Though he is not uncritical of their ways, neither does he want them to be changed. He regrets, for instance, that the children of 'Tony Widger' (Bob Woolley) are so well-fed, as Tony himself sometimes starved as a child, and this is what made him the man he became. Education of the working classes, he argues, turns boys into clerks and the girls into little snobs who desire piano lessons (the acquisition of pianos by the working classes is deplored by other observers such as Richard Jefferies). Reynolds's beliefs are spelt out more plainly in his book of 1911, *Seems So!*, for which his co-authors are said to be Bob and Tom Woolley. It is a 'true Collaboration' in which Reynolds has acted as secretary. Determinedly unintellectual, the book is full of homespun wisdom enlivened by occasional streaks of common sense: (there would, for example, be no need for tipping 'if people were paid proper'). Reynolds emerges as a sort of enlightened reactionary, his fellow-scribes as self-righteously opinionated. The suffragette or the 'gad-about girl' needs the curb of several children: '*they'll* tie her down and tame her'. Education is a waste of time; experience is the best teacher. The piano is once again the discordant instrument of empty refinery. In his need for the Woolleys, Reynolds desperately required them to stay the same, unchanged by progress: there's nothing here to make the establishment shake in their well-heeled shoes.

A Poor Man's House, where similar observations are strictly rationed, is a much better book, and was generally well-received. It was, wrote Conrad, 'compact' and 'harmonious'. Galsworthy praised the book too, and so did Arnold Bennett - but no one perhaps ever thought more highly of it than

Katie Powys. For her, Reynolds's book was 'the explanation of things simple and of things complex . . . It was the ladle by which I first sipped of the bowl of existence, passed on to me by the hands of men through long ages unknown. It carried an unseen power to buoy me up'.

Katie was in love; she had never before met anyone like Stephen Reynolds. When she talked with him he took her opinions seriously. As one of the youngest, and a highly-strung girl, in a large family, Katie was unused to having her views valued. She and Reynolds shared an admiration for the poems of Walt Whitman, and he introduced her to the works of Nietszche: Reynolds was her 'prophet' and her 'mentor'. Katie was an affectionate, impressionable young woman who had led a cloistered life of vicarage and governess. The world of literature, in which her brothers moved, was here presented to her by Reynolds and this, combined with the romantic background of fishermen and sea, was almost too exciting. She had found a new creed, one which was to last her the rest of her life. 'Not by the tarnished wood of dogma', she wrote, 'but by the tarred boats of fishermen should my soul tarry and find strength'.

Unhappily, Katie's love was not reciprocated. Reynolds showed little interest in women and apparently had no idea of Katie's feelings for him. In a fevered account of the affair in her prose-poem *The Phoenix* (or *Driven Passion*) she makes a return visit to Sidmouth, full of thrilled expectation. She meets Reynolds by chance and talks to him. When he remarks, perhaps in warning, during the course of the conversation that nature is his only friend, she is cut to the quick, her illusions abruptly, utterly destroyed. The result of this was that Katie suffered a severe nervous breakdown - she was, she wrote, 'thrown into the pit of madness' and was sent to a sanatorium in Bristol. The dizzying pain of the experience is evoked in *The Phoenix*.

Recovering slowly, Katie felt that she had become polluted, and she could never see Reynolds again. She had to learn to face the horror of this, that she is 'denied him even in dreams'. Reynolds himself, understandably enough, seems to have steered clear of what he had unintentionally unleashed. For the rest of her life, Katie kept an envelope marked 'Private. Steve's only letters to me - Katie Powys'. Inside are five short sheets, each one beginning 'Dear Miss Powys' and a single postcard with the message 'Very glad to hear you are so much better', signed 'S.R.' These dutiful missives are creased and fingered, treasured documents carefully preserved. A sixth letter, longer and written with gentle tact, was kept always in Katie's copy of Whitman's poems - frail mementoes all, but infinitely precious. It seems unlikely that Katie ever saw Reynolds again, and he died in the Spanish flu epidemic of 1919, yet as late as 1939 she is noting in her journal 'Steve's birthday'. By his death he became more securely hers, and she can refer to him as an established fact.

51. Katie Powys in Sidmouth with Bob Woolley.

The experience altered her life. For ever afterwards her family were both wary and protective of her nervous sensibilities. Much of Katie's personal consolation was to be found through landscape and weather. While she was ill, the sound of the winds was reassuring to her, 'thus the great winds became my lover and my God'. Like Whitman, she could feel herself a part of the natural forces, transcending the everyday world and at the same time being unified with it. Discarding orthodox religion, Katie placed her faith in nature - in that, and the cult of the fisherman. There is, in her brother Theodore's *Mockery Gap*, a gloriously divine fisherman who could almost have arisen from Katie's own writings.

The sun . . . set a burning and a shining match to the fisherman's hair, that seemed at that moment to be on fire; while his limbs, white and still glistening with drops from the sea, appeared to belong, by reason of their perfect proportion, to some high spirit from above rather than to a plain, though unnamed, fisherman from those islands.

135

This is a rare sighting for Theodore, but fishermen appear frequently in Katie's work. In her journals she quotes the sayings of the fisherman of Confucius (as well as those of Stephen Reynolds). She wrote two novels, *Further West* and *The Path of the Gale* as well as a verse-play, *The Quick and the Dead*, about them. There are poems, too, like 'Son of a Smuggler' in which the fisherman hero is seen to be 'keeping aloof with the pride of the proudest', and 'The Seaman'. Again, in an unfinished story, *To Conquer Madness*, a poignant blend of autobiography and wishful thinking, a young mad girl is sent to a remote place overlooking the sea. The doctor who counsels this cure for her illness also recommends a simple diet - and the offer of a reward to any man 'who would dare approach her as a lover'. As the girl is lodging at a fisherman's cottage, it is not difficult to guess what the outcome will be.

After her breakdown, though, Katie first went back to the land. She had, before her illness, been working along with Lucy on her brother William's farm at Witcombe near Montacute: In 1913 she attended agricultural college at Studley, Warwickshire, and by the summer of 1914 had joined a women's cooperative at Holban's Farm, Heathfield in Sussex. She then rented a small dairy close to Montacute, Roper's Farm, Stoke sub Hamdon. Katie's reminiscences of her farming adventures, written in the third person, have the breathless enthusiasm of a girls' school story. 'Some are called by the sea but this was the call of the land. She could not resist it. She had been reared by the meadows. Her spirit had drawn from them, so she longed to try her fortunes in the amiable breast of nature. There was an untold fascination in it. She knew there might be hardships . . . ' The cheerful tone suggests a good recovery from her illness and an excited pride in her achievement. 'She was now the owner of 8 cows, 2 horses and 32 acres rented from the landowner. Yes she was really an acknowledged farmer.'

Katie continued to farm until 1923. It was, as she had predicted, hard work, but she enjoyed the regular task of milking. In 1922, as a result of a fall from her horse, she had to have her teeth extracted, and this painful episode may have brought about the decision to give up the farm. Like her brother Theodore before her, she regarded her agricultural experiment as a failure. In April 1927 she wrote sadly, 'my farming has failed; and as I am slow and uncertain in my writing it is of no commercial value. Thus the good my life is to mankind is nil'.

Katie was here re-opening her journal after years of silence. Unfortunately she seems to have left no record of a happier time: the visit to America which she made not long after giving up the farm. In November 1923, she arrived in New York to stay in Patchin Place with her adored brother Llewelyn and his companion, Alyse Gregory, whom he was to marry the following year. Brother and sister would work side by side in New York Public Library, or sit together by the hour on a deserted wharf 'looking over the grey waters of the East River', away from the hectic vitality of life in the streets. They went, Llewelyn tells us in *The Verdict of Bridlegoose*, at Katie's instigation to a performance by the 'famous prophet and musician' Gurdjieff whose apostle, Orage, came to tea one afternoon in Patchin Place. Brother and sister were overjoyed to see one another again. 'It is lovely to feel her arms like iron bands around me', Llewelyn wrote. Alyse thought that Katie found the trip 'one of the great liberating experiences of her life' and certainly photographs from that period show Katie with a glowing and animated face (though clad in a much-hated dress, of velvet with ermine trimmings). America was to her enhanced by being the birthplace of Walt Whitman.

Katie spent four months in New York. On her return in April 1924 she and her eldest sister, Gertrude, who had cared for their father until his death, moved into Chydyok Farm. Freed from this duty, Gertrude took on the care of her sister. Although Katie could be over-emotional and awkward, Gertrude seems not to have minded this new responsibility. As the eldest sister of the family, it was assumed to be her place to care first of all for her ageing parents in Montacute, then after her mother's death in 1914, for her father in Weymouth (assisted by Theodore who made regular visits from Chaldon).

Gertrude had left Montacute temporarily to study painting, first attending the Slade School of Art where Alyse Gregory said 'she acquitted herself so brilliantly' that she was able to miss out a year's tuition, and then going on to Paris, from where she was recalled in 1914. She resumed her studies, again in Paris, shortly after her father's death in 1923. This was a less successful experiment, and she soon returned to England to look after another ailing relative, her Aunt Dora. After she moved in with Katie she continued to visit Paris and to paint. Her paintings, perhaps because of studies interrupted at such a crucial period, are unremarkable, except as a record of a time and a place.

Beautiful, stately and independent, Gertrude somehow managed to act as a mother figure to many of her brothers and sisters, and she was always very close to Theodore. Katie was the most vulnerable of her charges, as Alyse Gregory was later to appreciate. Left at Chydyok after Gertrude's death with only Katie for a neighbour, Alyse wrote to Valentine Ackland,

'I realise now how Gertrude used to protect her, I used to think she did it too much, but I understand why now'. Alyse came to value Gertrude more and more, propping up her photograph in her Devon room so that it was the last thing she saw before she died. Alyse has left, too, a ruefully funny account of Katie's attempts to use the telephone, with which she wrestled 'as if she were trying to pull up a runaway cart horse, six runaway cart horses, or hold up a falling building . . ' Katie battled not only with telephones but with 'Primuses, broom handles . . . bureau drawers, rugs, books, dust, hoes and flints'.

52. Katie and Gertrude Powys.

Gertrude, meanwhile, kept bees (in a glass box in the bedroom according to Nancy Cunard), grew flowers and fruit, planted trees, made wine and bread and lived a life of apparent serenity. Her diaries, inscrutably conventional documents, show exasperation only when her household routine is disrupted. How much she resented (if she did) her family burden is hard to judge. She had, Alyse Gregory wrote, 'a sense of responsibility, an extremely strong will, and a sense of compassion strongest of all'. Her next surviving sister, Marian, saw clearly that the same fate might befall her too, and made deliberate plans of escape. In 1913 she landed in America, found work as a typist and settled in New York State. She had studied lace-making in Europe, which she continued to practise in the evenings until the award of a gold medal in the Panama Pacific Exposition enabled her to open a lace shop, first of all in Washington Square. In 1922 she gave birth to a son, Peter Powys Grey, said to be the child of a journalist who then died of malaria in Italy. Gertrude was devoted to this nephew. In 1948 whilst staying at Chydyok, Peter Grey married Barbara Tyler in Chaldon church. Peter Powys Grey had fond memories of Gertrude and of Katie too, with her 'wild faults and gooseberry sweet virtues'.

At Chydyok, Katie (or Philippa, as she sometimes called herself) rode her pony Josephine, grew vegetables, walked on the downs and headlands, gathered driftwood or beachcombings from the shore and worked at her writing. She worked hard at it. Her poems, or those undated, disordered typescripts of them that remain, are carefully revised. Written in consciously poetic language they are often Whitmanesque, though with less originality of expression. Katie's poem 'Song of the Wind' opens with the words:

> Blessed is the wild rough weather,
> Blessed is the whistle of the wind,
> Blessed indeed is the wind that hath the breath of life:
> Blessed is the Spirit that joins its voice to that of the wind;
> Blest again is the Spirit that hears the voice and cannot reach it,
> Blessed above all are they, for they suffer not alone but in sympathy.

This poem was probably written in Chaldon. The Rat's Valley, the cliffs and Chydyok Farm are the inspiration and setting for many of the poems, which often seem to have been written in the heat of the moment. Heartfelt and eager, 'O!' they begin, or 'Behold!' The writer is conscious that this is the occasion for a poem. They are not faked; there is no doubting the strength of the poet's emotions. Mostly they seem the work of a very young person, especially in religious poems like 'Hallowed Ground' about an order of nuns who have taken a vow of silence - an incongruous piece for a creature like Katie who, 'born a heretic' had early lost faith in Christianity, regarding it as an obstacle to any true spirituality.

But Katie also possesses the intensity of youth, and her best poems are often those in simple and direct response to her surroundings. Her observation is close, yet unmyopic, as in 'On Awakening'.

> Sea winds moan,
> Thin light ascends
> Wrapt in shade;
> Sheep bells ring
> 'Mid the clamour of gulls.
> The lone moon broods
> Sinking to earth.
> Night winds have lifted.
> Frail mists disperse.
> Beneath and distinct
> The valley stands clear.

53. Katie and Josephine on Chaldon Down. Oil painting by Gertrude Powys.

In another quiet poem, 'The Under-Cliff', the writer is wondering (as Emily Bronte might) 'Who is there, if I am not there?/ When the rays of the autumn sun/ Light upon the bramble wild,/ Clustered full with chosen fruit'. By the poem's end this green longing has been reciprocated: the poet's hands are 'stained in blood,/ By the jealous bramble thorn'.

'The Under-Cliff' is among the poems included in the collection called *Driftwood* which was published in 1930. From this collection too, comes 'The Valley', a place forever sun-blest, moon-haunted, here recreated in a thorny irregular metre. Companion to the poem is an unpublished powerful short story of Chaldon, 'The Valley by the Sea' in which a man returns after a long absence to this seasoned valley, '. . . the whole place appeared welted from the effects of the wind and rain. The air was charged with salt. The smell of stranded sea-weed penetrated his senses. He became further aware of pieces of twigs and black leaves strewing the ground against bales and ditches'. The man is to be disappointed; his girl, he finds, has died in childbirth of another man's baby. The theme of disappointed return is a recurrent one in Chaldon lore, from the legend of the inn sign to Theodore's short story 'In from Spain' and the return of Fred in *Innocent Birds*. It was clearly unwise to leave the village.

Other poems record Katie's other loves. Valentine Ackland first visited the village in 1925, brought there by her friend Rachel Braden. Katie was attracted to both of them but more enduringly to 'Molly' as Valentine was then often known. It seems, over the next few years, that Molly sometimes responded but, being herself much admired, she was fickle and testing. Katie, generously loving and passionately single-minded, was ill-equipped to deal with this situation. She was made to feel clumsy and rejected. When Valentine began living in the village with Sylvia Townsend Warner, Katie found the situation intolerable. In about 1931 she wrote to Llewelyn, 'Molly is lost like the sun behind cloud. I hear nothing of her - sunless through Sylvia - This is distressing and tantalising'. Sylvia had blighted all her hopes. For years Katie found it difficult to be civil to Molly's friend, however kind Sylvia tried to be; only when they spoke of Theodore were they truly at ease.

One-sided, always passionate, Katie's love affairs were never easy. Indeed the recipients of her affection were sometimes made uneasy by the strength of her demands. She was deeply devoted to Llewelyn, her 'Brother of Brothers', confessing to him that when he was away 'my love for you becomes almost [more] excessive than I can bear'. Whether he was away or at home, it was not so much Llewelyn as Theodore who listened to Katie and steadied her. In 1930 she notes in her journal that Theodore has 'explained and straightened out a lot of my private problems . . . ' Llewelyn loved her too, but he had another partner, one whom fortunately Katie loved and accepted. Alyse Gregory's *Notes on C.E.P.P.* form the basis of this present account of Katie's life.

For her part, Alyse seems to have been fond of Katie. She has left a portrait of her sister-in-law in her novel *Hester Craddock*, as a clumsy and passionate creature, destroyed by unrequited love. Alyse helped Katie, by editing and influence, to get some of *The Phoenix* published in *The Dial*, a journal of which she had formerly been the managing editor. Other than *Driftwood* and four poetry pamphlets, Katie's only published work was her novel, *The Blackthorn Winter*. This, the story of Nancy Mead, a dairymaid betrothed to the blacksmith Walt Westmacott, is very much of its time, that of D. H. Lawrence's *The Woman Who Rode Away* and *The Virgin and the Gipsy* (Nancy runs away with a Romany). Naturally romantic, the book remains sturdily realistic in its descriptions of nomadic life. Nancy agrees to join her gypsy, Mike, at Bridgwater Fair and the first night of the elopement is spent, uncomfortably, in a caravan, where she is kept awake by the fairground noise and chaperoned by Mike's grandmother. Mike may be darkly attractive, but he's also violent and fond of drink. Nancy, too, unlike many a fictional dairymaid, is one who really (like Katie) knows the work. In *The Blackthorn Winter* the country scenes are freshly drawn.

One section of the book is enacted on the Dorset cliffs, with the Bay of Portland 'a silver shield' in the distance. From Dagger's Gate to Sea Barn the gypsy tracks are still to be seen, some of them now a regimented part of the coastal path. (The gypsies used the old Five Marys route as well, visiting the village to sell clothes pegs or, at Christmas, mistletoe.) In 1927 Katie noted that there was an encampment on the cliff from where she had 'picked out of the ashes of the fire a spoon'. When evoking similar scenes in her novel of places she knew well, Katie's writing is often at its best. And the tracks were soon to become for her more significant still. Whilst walking along them in the early 1930s, Katie encountered Jack Miller, who was out checking his rabbit snares. Jack was full of a youthful vitality and he was, of all things, a fisherman. Katie had never ceased to have the highest regard for this calling. She had bought Portland Cottage, Sidmouth, in 1930, an old house 'Lost in a courtyard, 'gainst a chapel wall', and she stayed there often, going out in the boats or running a tea-stall for the fishermen. She brought Bob Woolley and sometimes his son, Bill, on week-long trips to Chaldon. She found Bob easy company; with him, instead of shrinking away as she felt she often did, she was like 'a ship in full sail'. Bob was her link with Reynolds, and when he had a heart attack in 1927 she waited anxiously for his recovery. 'He is the half that's left of Stephen', she wrote.

54. The old Gypsy track above the cliffs.

But Jack Miller was probably the one who responded most to Katie. She wrote in her journal, 'Jack Miller/ Brown lover I met up on the hills/ He loved me most/ we lay together below Orion'. The hills, the secret remotenesses of Rat's Barn, were their meeting-places. A letter of 1933 from Jack to the absent Katie cheerfully recalls 'the Happy times we have spent'. 'I don't go through the Warren much now, as you know', Jack wrote. 'I am very timid, and I have no young lady to meet'. Jack's response was a generous one. Katie thought that 'No one I have ever fancied has turned to me with such over-bounding love. At last I have the mutual love of a man . . . sometimes I fancied I am embraced by some god in the garb of a fisherman . . . I rejoice!'

Katie, though, was ever unlucky in love. In March 1939, Jack, who had been helping to widen the Lulworth road all winter, was suddenly taken ill. Katie rushed to report the news to his Chaldon relatives, returning to his Lulworth home to find him dead (his crippled sister, strangely enough, was to die the next night). Katie saw Jack in his coffin and wrote that she 'cried out like an animal in pain'. At the Requiem Mass (Jack was a Catholic) it rained, and Katie was a little consoled when Mrs Lucas observed, 'More blessed is the corpse the rain rains on'.

Afterwards Katie wrote, 'Never shall I forget the addition Jack has made to my life here and it is hard, hard to resign myself to the knowledge that it is over. The garden, the paths, the Warren especially at night all bring back . . . his personality and the unique friendship he gave to me.'

Her consolation was as always in nature and in her life at Rat's Barn. She was ill after Jack's death (which was followed in December by Llewelyn's) and in 1940 Theodore sent a letter giving thanks for her recovery. He is glad she can go once more to the Barn 'and the flint stones and the chalk stones that lie about under the wall, and under the trees in the garden must be glad too'. Mentally she remained fragile. In 1949, Sylvia Townsend Warner noted in her diary that 'It is only a few who are transported to madness, the rest have to stumble towards it, over the soggy misleading ground, & through the obstacles of being a nuisance to those who love them, & a laughing-stock to strangers. Philippa's indifference to being comical & conspicuous shows how far she has been along that road . . . '

55. Memorial stone in the south west corner of Chaldon churchyard.

In her journals Katie has left a vivid portrait of herself and of the people and places she loved with the exceptionally deep love of which she was capable. Unpublished, her journals perhaps contain the best of her writing, free as they are from the artistic constraints of which she was so aware in work produced for eyes other than her own.

Katie was always popular in the village, and was remembered with great affection. She would sit on the barrels in the pub with the men, smoking Gold

Flake and drinking, devil-may-care. She felt at home down in Chaldon amongst her friends, and was particularly devoted to Alice Hewlett, herself the mother of six children, who had a maternal fondness for Philippa. In 1939, Katie noted, 'I am happiest when I am with Alice and Jim Hewlett drinking in the Sailor's Return, for I don't have to exert myself with them'. A stronger tribute is to be found in the draft of her will, where she stipulated that she wished to be buried 'as near as possible to my friend Alice Hewlett the wife of Jim Hewlett in the church yard of Chaldon Herring'.

This wish was to be fulfilled after Katie's death in the cold and snowy winter of 1963. Alice's grave is unmarked, but close beside it is a peeling wooden cross, bearing the initial 'K.P.' Close beside, as they also wished to be, are the ashes of Sylvia Townsend Warner and Valentine Ackland under a single stone which bears the words 'Non omnis moriar' (death is not the end).

Sylvia Townsend Warner had met Theodore Powys in Chaldon Herring. There, too, she was to meet Valentine Ackland who became her life-long companion. Valentine first came to the village in 1925, brought by her friend Rachel Braden, herself a friend of Stephen Tomlin. Valentine, then aged nineteen, was in wretched state. In the midst of a prolonged love affair with a young woman called Bo Foster, she had agreed to marry Richard Turpin, a blond young man as much at dazed odds with the prevailing sexual order as his future wife. Both were taking instruction in the Catholic faith. Given their youth, the almost accidental quality of their marriage, and their individual sexual inclinations, it was hardly surprising that their (delayed) wedding night was a failure. Eventually, Valentine had an operation to remove her hymen. She came to Chaldon to recover - and to escape from Richard.

The arrival of Valentine and Rachel, both clad in men's grey flannel trousers, must have caused something of a stir as it had done in Mecklenburgh Square, W.C. 1. They stayed together at No.17, Mrs Wallis's, along with Valentine's tortoise, who on their second visit got lost in the garden. The tortoise buried itself and was given up as lost until one morning when Valentine and Rachel were woken up by Mrs Wallis's excited voice shouting, 'Quick! Quick! Mrs Turpin's fish be come back'. 'Molly' as Valentine was then known (her given names were Mary Kathleen Macrory Ackland; she chose the name Valentine from a Loeb classic) was taken by Rachel to see Llewelyn and Alyse at their coastguard's cottage on the White Nose. They also went to Chydyok to see Gertrude and Katie, who were both admirers of Rachel, Gertrude later painting Rachel's portrait. She was an astonishing creature who, Valentine wrote, belonged to 'the near-stage people; the people who knew People. She was extremely attractive; slender, supple, boyish; completely amoral and very amorous'. She introduced Valentine as well to Theodore and Violet. Valentine for a while almost worshipped Theodore (so much so that her mother suspected he had seduced her daughter!) and Violet cared for her with a protective kindness. At the time of Violet's death in 1966, Valentine recalled to Alyse, 'I remember sitting at her feet while Theodore read aloud to her and Doris and me, one winter night, and she stroked my head and I suddenly thought, "This is like having a mother" . . . She could show great tenderness, and naturally, unselfconsciously . . . so that even my half-raw, half-sophisticated shyness was not alerted'.

56. Valentine Ackland by Eric Gill, c.1925, charcoal on paper.

A queasy insecurity is revealed in a reading of almost any letter of Valentine's and in her personal, enigmatic life-statement *For Sylvia* which, judging by its speculations about the effect the book will have on library borrowers, she did intend for publication. Yet Valentine had the worldly confidence to engage in many love affairs - even after her meeting with Sylvia - with both men and women, and some of these took place in Chaldon. By Christmas 1926 she was pregnant, though the child was not her husband's. She succeeded in getting her marriage annulled for non-consummation whilst in this state, such was the perfunctory nature of the medical examination. She dearly wanted a child and was bitterly upset when she miscarried at around four months, after slipping down a bank. Here again, Violet was a comfort to her. One of her admirers was Betty Muntz's cousin, Sydney Sheppard, who was an 'exciting lover' as Valentine was later to recount to Alyse. She told Alyse too, in later years, about her experiences in lesbian brothels in Paris and Hanover Square. She once, and once only, made love with Rachel, enjoying a 'very very brief, belated night together in [Rachel's] cottage at West Chaldon'.

On her first visits to Chaldon, Valentine would stay in one of the cottages, Mrs Wallis's or Mrs Legg's. On summer days she would go to Ringstead and sunbathe naked on the beach, walking back over the hills. Sometimes evenings were spent at Beth Car, where she would 'play soldiers with Violet and Doris, and then read aloud to Theodore, or roll spills while he read aloud to us all'.

Valentine was exceptionally tall, thin and dapper, careful of her appearance. In a letter to Katie of 1926 she describes a new golden-brown pair of corduroys and a gold and silver tie. Her fashionably long and graceful body, her 'weasel grace', was often sketched by Elizabeth Muntz and, in London, by Eric Gill. An admiration that was more difficult to handle was Katie's. After Katie's death Alyse looked through her journals, finding them as she told Valentine '*painful* reading - so much taken up with you - I could feel behind all your predicament - in the evasions and generous efforts *to do your best* - but her heart was always hungry . . . and every little attention handed out to her became a major delight'.

Katie's frail hopes were finally dashed when Sylvia Townsend Warner became central to Valentine's life. The couple first met at one of Valentine's tea parties. Long afterwards, Sylvia recalled that Valentine had been 'tall, slender as a willow-wand, sweet scented as a spray of Cape Jessamine, almost as silent, too'. Sylvia felt that she was herself 'none of these things', and that her conversation had been 'aggressively witty and overbearing'.

Despite this inauspicious beginning, Valentine was to offer Sylvia the use of her cottage whilst she was away. Although Sylvia declined, the landlord came to hear of the offer and turned Valentine out for sub-letting.

As the unwitting cause of Valentine's eviction, Sylvia, on Violet's suggestion, bought 'the late Miss Green's' cottage and in her turn invited Valentine to live there, saying that she could keep an eye on the house whilst Sylvia was absent.

57. Studio photograph of Sylvia Townsend Warner by Howard Costner.

Sylvia moved into Miss Green's, which had been freshly decorated with white walls and pink woodwork, on October 4th, 1930. Valentine arrived in the evening and they dined on duck - which had taken hours to cook, thanks to the new oven - and a giant field mushroom picked on the Five Marys. They dined in some style. Unusually for a Chaldon cottage, Miss Green's was equipped with such trappings as an oval mirror, Regency teaspoons and porcelain coffee cups. '. . . we declared against the grated carrot, folk-pottery way of life. Outside the quiet room the wind from the sea blew in gusts. We sat in our cocoon of warmth and subdued light and it seemed odd that we had not been living there for years'.

One week later, they made a fruitless effort to intercede on behalf of the servant girl at the old Vicarage, who had just made two attempts to escape. Their failure to have any influence on Mrs Stevenson saddened and enraged Valentine and later that night, when they were in their separate bedrooms at Miss Green's, they began to talk through the thin walls about human relationships. Suddenly Valentine said, 'Sometimes I think I am utterly unloved.'

I jumped out of bed, in a flash. I was through the door and on my knees at her bedside, crying out that it was not true, not true, that she must not say such a thing. She gathered me up in an embrace to lie beside her.

So began a marriage that was to last until death. The next morning, Sylvia wrote in her diary, was 'a bridal of earth and sky, and we spent the morning lying in the hollowed tump of the Five Maries, listening to the wind blowing over our happiness'. The Five Marys became a special landmark for them, like the solitary thorn on the Drove and the line of young ash trees which bordered their garden.

Both women have left tributes to the happiness they shared in the house. In 'The Death of Miss Green's Cottage' Sylvia wrote:

> The little house, so harmless and demure.
> I am glad to think that on its last day it wore
> Its laundered garden, its loved look, as when in love we were there.

Valentine describes their growing love in *For Sylvia*. When Miss Green's was destroyed she told Alyse Gregory, 'In that house I was as happy as I have ever been or ever can be; happier, I think, than I have ever been - for it was the least anxious of my pleasure and joy that I have ever known'. At Miss Green's they shared 'a wise, fantastic, passionate and fulfilled love'.

They were well-matched. It was Valentine who drove the two-seater car - and with great pleasure - who dealt with the practicalities, and who put an end to their much-loved animals when they became old or ill. Sylvia, a published writer, and a naturally happier and more confident person, gave Valentine the love and security she needed. Sylvia, Valentine confided to lylse, had 'a wonderfully good character and almost never has black and desperate despairs'. Early on, Valentine had shown Sylvia, at the latter's request, some of her poetry. Sylvia commented - rather evasively - that they were like pebbles 'weighted with intention', 'sleeked and shaped by the workings of a restless mind'.

58. Valentine Ackland outside No 24 with Vicky the goat.

She encouraged Valentine's writing and in 1934 they published a joint book of poems entitled *Whether a Dove or Seagull*. The poems are not individually attributed (except by a list in the back of the collection), the idea being that 'by withholding individual attributions on the page [the authors] hope that some of the freshness of anonymity may be preserved'. The book is thus a protest against those who judge a poem by the poet. It was, Sylvia later remarked, a 'vain gesture', made the vainer, one would think, by allowing attributions in the back of the book.

The gesture was a political, as much as an artistic one. Since the poems are mainly a lovers' dialogue, the form helps to protect love's privacy, but the ostensible reason for anonymity, for avoidance of the individual gesture, was a Communist one. Sylvia Townsend Warner has said that she became a Communist in 1933 after the Reichstag Fire Trial. She and Valentine were admitted to the party in the spring of 1935, and they were both much involved with the Republican cause in the Spanish Civil War. Valentine collected in the village, there were public meetings in Dorchester for Spain and for the Labour cause, at which John Cowper Powys spoke (in a speech on behalf of the Republican cause he talked for half an hour on personal happiness). Perhaps through Valentine, Katie too became involved. Sylvia and Valentine went to Barcelona for three weeks in 1936 and to the Second International Congress of Writers in Defence of Culture in 1937.

Party members visited Chaldon, where the two women were producing a mass of letters and articles, both on behalf of the Spanish Republicans and of the other left-wing causes closer to home. Even Theodore was recruited (if not press-ganged). One of his contributions - to a fund-raising pamphlet called *Spain and Us* - was a kind of Hispanic hermit's soliloquy.

59. Sylvia and fellow-Communists at 24 West Chaldon.

What is it all for? Here is a simple-minded nation - Spain - where, I used to say, the last gentleman might be found, riding a donkey upon his threshing-floor to tread out his wheat and barley; where a village could be yet a village, with a friendly heap of bones under the churchyard wall to tell one that man is mortal. Now here are these simple good-humoured people, old women, pretty children, and cows, made a target of as if they were so many Aunt Sallies at a fair to be battered into unsightly carrion at the pleasure of devils.

Spanish Burgundy is a very good cheap wine, that can fill one with peace and content, but how can peasants attend to their vine dressing when they meet more bullets than grapes, more bombs than pruning-hooks? The world has come to this - unless my neighbour can have his will of me, spike me with a sharp sword, turn me out of my garden like another Adam, march me up and down until I learn to hold up my hands as if I were carelessly crucified, I am a socialist, an incendiary, one of the red rabble, to be destroyed at his pleasure.

Were ever poor sinners more betrayed than the innocents of this world?

Back in Chaldon, Sylvia and Valentine were also concerning themselves with more local matters. Sylvia became secretary of Dorset Peace Council in 1936, and both women were founder members of a Readers' and Writers' group. Valentine, who was of a far more religious bent than her lover (and who would eventually rejoin the Catholic faith, to Sylvia's dismay) was probably the more fervent of the two.

In 1935, Valentine wrote a series of articles called 'Country Dealings' for the *Left Review*. These, based on her close observation of village life in Chaldon and in Norfolk, were collected as *Country Conditions* in 1936. The book tells in damning detail of the neglected conditions of several neighbouring cottages - those of Fred Dory, labourer; Jack Ensor, carpenter; and Joe Talbot, labourer. These are all village names: Joe Talbot, 'Permit-of-Exemption' man, who walks with a limp and has an ailing wife, is most probably based on Jim Pitman, whose living conditions improved when he became tenant at Miss Green's.

Valentine believed that the existing social system was largely to blame for the state of the buildings. She and Sylvia challenged the prevailing order by a variety of actions, such as protesting to the Welds about their contaminated water (Sylvia found dead rats in the well), by ferrying villagers to the polling station one by one in Valentine's two-seater, so that they could vote labour, and by organising a celebration to rival the one held for the King's Jubilee in the village. Their anarchic variant included 'a bonfire on High Chaldon, fireworks, a burning cartwheel tumbled down the hillside . . . and a dance on the sward, with a barrel of very strong cider . . .' as Valentine described it to Hope Muntz.

So, for a little while, rather to the mistrust and bewilderment of some of the villagers, Chaldon Herring became red.

Yet despite her happiness in Chaldon, a secret shadowed Valentine's life. After the trial of her marriage, her shyness on social occasions, after the red wine prescribed for her as a specific for neuralgia and again for anaemia, she became addicted to alcohol. She describes her addiction, which lasted for nineteen years, in her autobiographical essay. For the

152

reader the puzzle is how alert, intelligent Sylvia, who lived with Valentine and was devoted to her, failed to notice the extent of her drinking. It seems likely that Valentine must have been exaggerating, self-dislike is draggling her account.

60. 'The Hut', 24 West Chaldon.

In 1933 Sylvia and Valentine took a temporary leave of Chaldon, renting out Miss Green's cottage, and moving to Frankfort Manor at Sloley in Norfolk. As a result of the expense of the Vicarage libel case (or because Frankfort was an experiment that somehow failed) they came back at Martinmas, 1934. They had been to Chaldon in the autumn of that year to talk to Llewelyn about the case, and, Sylvia wrote, 'The imperturbable familiar landscape, the landscape of our first love, called us back.' As Miss Green's was too small for permanent use, Sylvia and Valentine rented the cottage behind the Hut Dairy on the road between East and West Chaldon. Stately barns and lowly cottages were the natural order in Chaldon, and this was a characteristic group. The Hut Dairy survives in a gentrified style, but the cottage, like Miss Green's, has vanished. It lies 'stone on stone' recalling Nelly Trim's in Sylvia's poem, though outlasting Miss Green's by more than two decades. It was still there in 1963, as Lucy Penny (née Powys) told Sylvia, 'looking sadly derelict but *still occupied* - washing on the line, and a man came out of the house.' 'The Hut', No.24, was later pulled down by the farmer, James Cobb. Even in the 1930s it was in a sorry state.

'It had the outlook of a castle, it faced the south and winds smelling of the sea; we stepped out of it on to the untrammelled solitude of the downs. But it had no lighting, no sanitation, no damp-course, and eight dead rats were dredged from its well . . .' Both women developed stomach complaints and colds, and their belongings developed mildew. Fortunately they were young and active enough to disregard the worst of the discomfort, as Valentine related to Alyse.

Too well I remember returns to 24 West Chaldon, when no one had been there and the house was exhaling the smell of a tomb and the walls wept and the floors were like the floors of hell. In those days I was able to be aware of the hill outside and the great valleys and sometimes even of the cliffs and the sea beyond them . . .

61. Dust jacket for *Country Conditions,* 1936

On the hill of High Chaldon, Sylvia and Valentine would take their goat, Victoria Ambrosia, for walks. Sylvia was particularly fond of nocturnal walks. Both were deeply involved in their writing. Valentine wrote *Country*

Conditions up at Rat's Barn. Whilst staying there, she and Sylvia wrote to each other daily, as they were accustomed to do whenever they were apart. Sylvia now had a body of published work to her credit and was contributing to the *New Yorker*, as she was to do for more than forty years. Valentine too was 'well-thought of' in the thirties and forties as a writer, though later, Sylvia wrote, 'fell out of fashion', but these were still early days - and happy ones.

Valentine was not sexually faithful, but this did not trouble Sylvia: 'She was so skilled in love that I never expected her to forgo love-adventures. Each while it lasted (they were brief) was vehement and sincere. They left me unharmed and her unembarrassed.' Until, that is, Valentine fell in love with an American woman named Elizabeth Wade White in 1938. Apparently over by 1940, the affair was rekindled in 1949. Sylvia and Valentine agreed to a temporary separation, but before this was effected they returned to Chaldon early one July morning in 1949 and visited the ruins of Miss Green's in its summer-wild garden. As they were leaving the village, Sylvia caught sight of their blackthorn on the Drove, and she wept.

Sylvia was to visit Chaldon again on the seventh day of her 'ancient solitary reign', exiled in Yeovil. She stayed at Chydyok with Alyse, a woman who had known similar sorrows, and slept in Llewelyn's shelter. She slept, she wrote, 'in a charm, between the east and the west', her unhappiness temporarily assuaged. When she returned to Chydyok - with Valentine - in April of the following year, the affair was finally over. 'It was such intense happiness,' she wrote. Chaldon was once more for her a place of joy.

In 1961, Sylvia reflected on the village's alchemical qualities. 'Looking back on Chaldon, it seemed so rich, so richly pastoral, though it is poor country, thistles and flints. But richness of colouring, amplitude - amplitude of days, richness of feeling.'

Valentine for her part came to regard Chaldon as a lost Eden, a place for which she was homesick - and found painful to revisit - long after she had left. In 1944 she wrote to Alyse from Frome Vauchurch of the place 'where I have been happier and freer than in any place else - and where there is so *much* that I starve for here'.

As well as Theodore and Violet, Valentine was fond of some of the other villagers, like Mr Goult the carrier, Shepherd Dove and Annie Moxon. 'Grannie' Moxon lived in the cottage behind the Sailor's Return, No. 22 East Chaldon, described in the 1929 sale catalogue as 'very picturesque' with a 'good garden and a productive orchard'. Decidedly detached, it probably dates from the eighteenth century and had two rooms up, two rooms down and a single-storey thatched extension to the north. The garden looks fecund; in Grannie's day even the thatch was sprouting, and adders sunned themselves on the bank beside the house.

62. Granny Moxon's cottage today which has outwardly changed very little.

Stories, too, flourish at Annie Moxon's name. She was thought by the village children to be a witch, one of several in Chaldon. Others were old Mrs Way, of whose funeral in 1920 Theodore wrote, 'Such a little coffin . . . It was like a doll's funeral', and Bessie Cornick, who lived opposite the churchyard. She was a huge old lady, a smoker of Player's, and is apparently the model for 'Rebecca' in Sylvia's story 'Early One Morning' (from *The Salutation*). In the story the clergyman, Arthur Clay, is ill-at-ease with his parishioners, both the quick and the dead. Passing Rebecca's house one morning, he hears the voices of several of his flock, curiously coming from the hen-house. They have been transformed into fowls. Rebecca herself becomes a greyhound bitch, 'milk-white, and young'. She persuades Mr Clay to toll the bell - for old Rebecca, who is dead.

Less fanciful (and less like T. F. Powys) is Valentine's account of Bessie for the *West Country Magazine*. Here she is 'old Allie', a 'stout old woman who wore a round knitted cap'. She used to sweep out the church and ring the bell for services. It was her habit to play tricks on the villagers, working 'just hard enough . . . to keep people in awe of her'. When she died, a bottle was found halfway up her chimney, a charm perhaps to keep away the devil. Under her bed (and utterly unexplained) were ranks of clean jam jars. Allie had always lived well, though on what means no one knew, with lashings of food and tobacco. She was regularly called on to visit new-born babies, in order to predict their future health. It was said in the village that when she died, she was too large to carry down the cottage stairs (which may have been no more than a ladder). The upstairs or 'coffin' window had to be removed to get her body through.

Mild witches these, evidently losing their powers, or at least their vindictiveness, by this time. A few still had the ability to turn into hares. In an essay entitled 'Folk-lore in Dorset', Llewelyn Powys describes an authority on such matters, Mrs Toms of Ringstead, 'a tall raw-boned woman now in Owermoigne churchyard'. She told him of a witch who used to torment a local farmer. The farmer's troubles were ended when he shot a hare with a bullet made from a silver sixpence. Such a talent was attributed to Mrs Way, and people avoided her cottage (except for Theodore, who would go and read to her once or twice a week).

This was a common enough belief, found all over the British Isles, but not one, it seems, applied to Annie Moxon. She was perhaps marked out because of her differences, her 'old-fashioned ways': she was fearless, sage, uncritical, and full of life. Grannie Moxon kept bees and made mead, which was said by one observer to be 'magnificent' and by another as 'too dirty to drink'. She sold honey as well, and the occasional lump of beeswax to passing gypsies. She kept goldfinches in cages in her dark and crowded room, and used reddle (sheep-dye, probably obtained from the shepherd) to stain her earth floor. Most of her evenings were spent at the inn, where she would talk, tell stories or sing strange songs to the accompaniment of her accordion.

Much material on Mrs Moxon is supplied by Valentine Ackland, who obviously felt a strong kindred with her. Her feelings are explained in a letter to Alyse Gregory.

When Grannie Moxon was dying, almost was dead, I stood by her bed and held her hand. I was alone with her and she was conscious, and I said are you all right, Grannie? And she said, in that kind of rough tenderness of voice that she used towards me, which was a solace and comfort to me - 'I be all right' - and I asked if she was afraid, and she said No. And, greatly daring because I trusted her courage, I asked if she thought of God and she said 'Not I!'

A year before she and I and Sylvia had walked along to the Marys late one night, and Grannie, holding our arms, sang loudly. I was troubled at that time by fears of death, and I asked her what she thought, if she believed in immortality? She answered:- 'Why - I do know how they be laid in ground, don't 'un? and no one b'aint getting up no more be 'un?' I persisted, and she said finally, 'No, me dear, and that I don't. 'Tis into the ground wi'ee and done with, so 'tis.'

And she sent her laughing cry, like a woodpecker's, across the hill. I wish she had not died so soon. I felt more sharply a tie of mother-and-child with her than ever I felt before . . .

Again, in another account, Valentine wrote that when Mrs Moxon died the village was like a 'dead body . . . for she had been the spirit, incomprehensible, irreplaceable; gone no-one knows where'. Her death seems, for a while at least, to have affected Valentine's feeling for the village.

It affected Sylvia too. She wrote more than one elegy for Granny Moxon.

> 'Twenty times, I suppose, I've danced alone -
> And no one wagged a better bone
> Than I, in times gone by -
> But Oh - remembering freely, as I can,
> When first I had my man
> Clapped in my arms so neat and spry -
> No girl so glad as I!'

> 'No girl so glad as I -' she said -
> And like a jay's cry overhead
> Her laugh shrieked across the room -
> Strange that she's gone - and why? -
> To dark earth, lonely tomb -

Sylvia Townsend Warner also treats of Annie Moxon in an untitled poem from *Whether a Dove or Seagull*, describing 'she whom all/ Think witch, and call/ Grannie - though she goes light-foot as a girl/ Under her threescore years and ten'. Here, Grannie becomes exuberantly, not just the spirit of the village, but that of the earth, crowned by the sun's slanting rays as she battles, as ever, with her garden in the April dusk. Like Joseph Staines Cope, but with a more serious intent, Grannie Moxon becomes an exalted, almost mystical figure, in Warner's hands.

This poem could be regarded as the starting-point for another, more ambitious and complex work, *Opus 7*. Set in Love Green, the village of Warner's essay, the poem is written in versatile, well-sustained couplets, reminiscent of Crabbe, and once more features a 'Rebecca', a solitary old woman whose garden becomes a village attraction. Rebecca wantonly grows flowers, not stoutly sensible vegetables. She has a rare ability for producing them from stolen cuttings or from the wonders of Woolworth seed packets, bought in the market town. She sells the flowers to passers-by, to summer visitors, or for use at rural functions, using the proceeds to buy bottles of gin, which she drinks in regular nightly rituals.

63. Edward Bawden cover design for the Dolphin Books series.

Such is her success that two mortally ill villagers vie with one another to die first, as Rebecca's garden has flowers enough to bedeck only one grave. Rebecca strips her garden for the winner, Bet, then goes, on a wild night, to the public house to buy four bottles of gin with her earnings. Returning, she visits the graveyard (there is, thanks to T. F. Powys, a glut of graveyards in Warner's early work) and finds her flowers gone. There, among the tombstones, Rebecca teaches Bet and God a lesson by drinking herself to death.

Opus 7 (1931) was indeed Sylvia's seventh published work. Her second, the novel *Lolly Willowes*, perhaps speaks more than any other for the widow, the spinster, for all women whose lives, by accident or design, do not follow the conventional pattern, and who refuse to pay the penalty expected of them in the role of devoted relative, charity worker or general dogsbody. Lolly, having escaped from her position as spinster aunt by becoming a witch, tells Satan her master,

It's like this. When I think of witches, I seem to see all over England, all over Europe, women living and growing old, as common as blackberries, and as unregarded . . . there they were, there they are, child-rearing, house-keeping, hanging washed dishcloths on currant bushes . . . And all the time being thrust further down into dullness when the one thing all women hate is to be thought dull.

So they become witches, to satisfy the desire for adventure, to have a secret life of their own, a life to which excitement rather than duty is central. In an age when witchcraft had lost its deathly sting, a woman could safely cultivate the title of witch - or, if labelled as such for odd or individual behaviour, accept the same title as a grudging tribute. Either way, she would be rendered less than dull.

Elizabeth Muntz, the sculptor and long-term resident of Chaldon, was a person who did take what she considered her village duties seriously - and evidently gave and derived much enjoyment from doing so.

Born in Toronto, Elizabeth was of English and French descent. Her great-grandfather, George Frederick Muntz, M.P., was one of the early campaigners for the abolition of child labour. Elizabeth studied at Ontario College of Art and in Paris. Although also a painter, she was predominantly a sculptor in bronze, wood and, above all, stone. In London she worked, like Stephen Tomlin, under Frank Dobson, and Tomlin it was who suggested that she should go to Chaldon. She lived in No. 17, to which she gave the name Apple-Tree Cottage, and which she bought in the Weld Estate sale of 1929, one of the few purchases actually made in that time of slump. She had her studio in the end cottage of the row at the bottom of the garden, which was said to be the oldest dwelling in Chaldon, part-built from the hulk of a Spanish galleon (and formerly known as Ship's Timbers). She removed the ground-floor ceiling of the cottage and inserted new windows to increase the light. This cottage row, now painstakingly restored, is a charming huddle of little rooms, in which several people would once have lived. The middle house of the row was the home of Billy Lucas, his wife and sons, Harry and Leonard.

Cottage and studio are linked by gardens. In Elizabeth's day her garden was overgrown and studded with statues, examples of her work. She worked intently, energetically, exhibiting, like Gertrude Powys, with the London Group, and also abroad. Her first exhibition was on Selfridges's roof garden, and a bronze group of child with fawn stood permanently there until its destruction during the Second World War. Influenced by Eric Gill, she enjoyed lettering, but the human form was of the greatest interest in her work. She was particularly attracted by babies and young children, painting and modelling some of them, like Josie, the young daughter of Bob and Florrie Legg. In 1965 she illustrated a children's book *The Dolphin Bottle*, to a text by Elizabeth Sprigge.

64. Elizabeth Muntz art class on the cliff looking east towards Bat's Head.

Miss Muntz involved herself in other ways with the village children. Hanging in the church is an appliqué picture, which she designed during the war, and worked on with the children in her studio. The picture is an animal nativity, in which the beasts, all local characters, wander down from the Five Marys to worship the infant Jesus (see Pl.36). In her garden she had a thatched log cabin, 'Little Apples', a romantic playground for the children. For several years, too, Miss Muntz held a summer school at her house (or, in fine weather, on the cliffs) teaching sculpture, painting and pottery, and this is remembered as being very successful.

For much of the time her companion was a Frenchman called André Bonnamy, whom she met in London art circles. Bonnamy had a caravan in the garden and would help Elizabeth with practical tasks. When money was running low, he would make a trip to London and find work as a technical translator. He died within a year of Miss Muntz, and their gravestones stand side by side in the churchyard. His bears the inscription, 'L'humanité refait son âme plus avec ses mains qu'avec sa pensée'; hers, 'I will lift up mine eyes unto the hills'. On her stone she is described simply as 'Sculptor'.

If Elizabeth Muntz is to be remembered as a sculptor, other than locally, it will be for her versatile work in stone - Purbeck, Portland, and Ham. (She was the first female Freeman of the Ancient Order of Purbeck Marblers and Stonecutters.) Characteristically firm and thorough, her work was constructed on architectural principles, and was of particular interest to architects. Her most noticed work at the present time must be the head of Theodore Powys in the Dorset County Museum (which held a major retrospective of her work in 1971). This sculpture is, as the Stone Industries journal reports, a 'very simplified statement', but an impressively massive one.

Better is the memorial to Llewelyn Powys on the cliffs above Chydyok. This takes the form of a rough stone block on which Miss Muntz, who liked to work as far as possible in situ, carved his chosen epitaph. A photograph shows her, having ridden up on her pony Barleycorn, with tool-bag and duffel-coat, hard at work and heedless of the sea-winds blowing around her. It was a task she triumphantly completed.

Her tribute to the Chaldon Powyses was generous, they in their response were less enthusiastic (apart from Llewelyn, who was apt to be kindlier in his remarks on other people). In the village, though, Miss Muntz is remembered with affectionate respect. She died in 1977.

Elizabeth Muntz had known Chaldon for some fifty years. Another member of her family, Isabelle Hope Muntz, also spent some time in the village. Although she too had studied art in Toronto and London (and at one time worked in aircraft engineering), her career took a different course. Whilst in Chaldon, in her half-sister's studio, Hope Muntz completed her only novel, *The Golden Warrior*, the story (or saga) of Harold and William and their battle for the English crown. This is an honourable, scholarly work, based wherever possible on contemporary sources, an elaborate tapestry ranging over France and England (and through several editions, so successful was it). One scene is set on Chaldon village green. Hope Muntz's other major work was a translation, with her friend Catherine Morton, of one of those contemporary sources, *The Carmen de Hastingae Proelio* of Guy, Bishop of Amiens (Hope was especially interested in the Norman Conquest). Other writings appeared under the pseudonym of William Langland. Hope Muntz was elected a Fellow of the Society of Antiquaries in 1969 and of the Royal Historical Society in 1972. Her gravestone in Chaldon churchyard describes her, accurately enough, as 'Scholar and Author'. She died in 1981.

65. Hope and Elizabeth Muntz at Apple-Tree Cottage.

Katie Powys, her sister Gertrude, Valentine Ackland and Sylvia Townsend Warner, Hope and Elizabeth Muntz all lived, without husbands, childless in a village, yet succeeded in following, in this place of possibilities, their own individual ways.

While in Rat's Barn, uncomfortable and awkward of access, Katie Powys learnt, perhaps better than anyone, the rewards of fully facing the loneliness of life.

Chaldon Herring

The Ballad of Chaldon Down

She came to me by ditch and stile,
She came to me through heather and brake,
And many and many a flinty mile
She walked in April for my sake,
All for to say good-day to me.

She came by way of Lulworth Cove
She came by way of Diffey's Farm;
All in a green and silver frock,
With half its flounces over her arm,
By the Bat's Head at dusk she came,
Where inland from the Channel drove,
The fog, and from the Shambles heard
The horn above the hidden rock;

And startled many a wild sea-bird
To fly unseen from Durdle Door
Into the fog; and left the shore,
And found a track without a name
That led to Chaldon, and so came
Over the downs to Chydyok,
All for to say good-day to me.

Edna St. Vincent Millay.

CHAPTER SEVEN

Chydyok

Before making his home at Chydyok in 1931 alongside his sisters Katie and Gertrude, Llewelyn Powys lived for six years in one of the row of coastguard cottages a mile's walk away on the White Nothe headland. The White Nothe (or Nore) is known locally as the White Nose, a village variant for which Thomas Hardy once provided a brisk explanation. 'Of course it is White Nose, it always has been called White Nose. You can see if you look that the cliff is shaped like a nose. It is like the Duke of Wellington's nose'.

This palely patrician nose marks the last eastern outcrop of the chalk which stretches, in gleaming dips and swoops, from Worbarrow Bay to Lulworth Cove and Bat's Head. Beyond are the gault beds of Ringstead Bay and of Holworth Burning Cliff (so-called after it ignited in 1826). In *Dorset Essays* Llewelyn describes the White Nose, a place he knew as well as anyone, with its ravens nesting there long after they had become rare in the rest of the county, the hidden cave under the 'dense weight' of the cliff, the whitened groves of skeleton trees which litter the landslip. As a treatment for his tuberculosis he slept out in a shelter there, and had his study in a little stone house with a boat for a roof - a boat which had once belonged, it was claimed, to the smugglers, and was now as solidly leaded as any church tower.

The White Nose was perhaps Llewelyn's favourite place. As a child he had walked there from his grandmother's house in Weymouth and later, when he lay ill in the seaside town, he watched it from his window. He was no fair-weather lover of the cliffs; he knew them in all seasons. In an uncollected essay he describes the excitement of wintering there.

On White Nose cliff after a November gale I have often picked up sea-weed, though the top of the headland stands 600 feet above the waves. The winds there would be so violent as to blow in the windows of the coast-guard cottages and to send slates from our roof flying over the ploughlands behind the houses as lightly as though they were sycamore leaves. And then, as soon as ever the wind went down, a sea mist would suddenly descend upon us enveloping us utterly . . .

66. Fountain Rock and The White Nose.

When the storms were at their worst it was almost impossible to hear oneself speak.

There had been a Signal House on White Nose as early as 1811, and in the census of 1841 thirty-one people were listed as living in seven cottages. Forty years on there were twenty-seven people, coastguards and their families. The buildings were then, as Llewelyn remembered from his childhood, 'a row of firm one-storied wooden houses shining with pitch and white paint' - probably not unlike the old coastguard cottages still to be seen at Osmington Mills. By the time Llewelyn came to live at White Nose, the houses had been rebuilt. Behind a high wall, constructed to keep out the worst of the gales, they stand, a bleak brown barracks of a row, facing out over the changing sea, over the

67. The coastguard cottages. Llewelyn Powys & Alyse Gregory lived at No 6.

remains of war-time fortifications, vigilant as ever. In 1925, as now, they were almost entirely used as holiday houses. Llewelyn and Alyse became accustomed to often being the only occupants, though neighbours, even noisy ones, could have their compensations. On the ones who moved into the next-door cottage, Llewelyn wrote to Rivers Pollock, 'We have two girls next door with a gramophone and cars. The place is not the same. The girl is attractive though and for this reason I cannot be as splenetic as I wish to be. She hangs up on the line little silken meshes for supporting her little breasts which are as pleasantly shaped as any William pears on your garden wall . . . '

The White Nose was home to Llewelyn, but it was a new world for his wife whom he had met and married in America. Alyse Gregory, managing editor of an important literary magazine, *The Dial*, had invited Llewelyn, whose work was gradually becoming recognised in the United States, to tea in her rooms in Patchin Place, New York. Before long Llewelyn was living there with her and they married, rather to Alyse's reluctance, in 1924. As a feminist she regarded marriage with some unease, and insisted on keeping her own name. Her journal for Oct.1, 1924 gives expression to her feelings.

Yesterday was my wedding day. It is what L. wanted, but some cloud lies upon my spirit as if I had betrayed something in myself . . . What should I fear? Only one fear I have, that he will cease to love me as he does. I must always be prepared for this, though he thinks this wounding to his illusions. But he is loved by every woman . . .

If Alyse's uneasiness extended to the move to England then she does not say so, even though this meant the virtual end of her career. 'It's disgraceful of me to have persuaded Alyse to give up *The Dial* but I WANT TO COME HOME' Llewelyn wrote to Gertrude. Unfortunately, too, Alyse's journal makes no mention of her first impressions of a place which could hardly have been more different from New York (though she had been to England at least twice before). With Llewelyn beside her, whatever her initial reaction, Alyse soon came to appreciate her changed environment, and her journals record the sea birds, the first viper's bugloss, the heavy horses harnessed three together in the fields. At White Nose they were not, in fact, living in particularly primitive conditions. When the poet Marianne Moore, who succeeded Alyse as editor of the *Dial*, came to visit them, she thought the house 'the embodiment of poetic scholarly seclusion. A lion's skull rests on each side of the book case in the dining room. Flowers and fruit in profusion on the side board and the china & silver are dainty and elegant and indigenous.' Nor were they as cut off as the location suggests (except in the sense that the houses had no water). Gertrude and Katie were living at Chydyok, Theodore was in the village, there were often plenty of visitors. One visitor was Llewelyn's friend Bernie O'Neill, others were his brother Bertie and niece Isobel, who came with the writer Naomi Mitchison. Mrs Mitchison gave a fictionalised account of the journey in her novel *The Corn King and the Spring Queen*, and also described the visit in her autobiography, *You May Well Ask*.

I can't not remember Llewelyn Powys, the first time, driving with beautiful Isobel, his niece, behind the clopping horse through winding roads to the windy house, high up, and then the talk, cautious at first, then easy and warm, reaching out tentacles towards further closeness. For a few years I saw a lot of Lulu; together we watched the fox family in the undercliff below the chalk and smelt sun-soaked whin and sea spray. I wish now I had made love with him, as he wanted, but somehow it didn't work in my own life . . .

68. Llewelyn Powys at the White Nose.

A visitor during Llewelyn's and Alyse's second stay at the White Nose in 1927 was an American friend of theirs, Walter Franzen. He went out walking one day and failed to return. All afternoon and evening Llewelyn, Alyse and Katie searched the headlands, scanning the empty beaches for a sign of him. Finally they made their way to Rose Cottage, Ringstead, and asked Harry Miller the fisherman to take his boat out in a search under the cliffs.

Sleepless, at 5 o'clock in a May dawn, they stood high above and watched as Harry Miller approached West Bottom, the promontory to the east of the White Nose, and then disappeared behind Fountain Rock. When he reappeared, Harry Miller carried in his boat - his 'carriage of death' - the body of Walter Franzen. Later Franzen's walking-stick and towel were found, the latter 'wrapped about like the sepulchral napkin of our Lord and laid neatly in a safe place' as Llewelyn wrote in a letter to John Cowper Powys.

This accident (there was no suggestion of suicide) is sorrowfully evoked in one of Llewelyn's best essays, 'A Grave in Dorset' a muted tolling for Franzen's unexpected death. Sadly, such accidents are not uncommon; the coast is dangerous. The following year, Katie noted in her journal that Harry Miller had found the body of another man at Osmington.

Franzen's funeral procession drew slowly across the valleys from the headland to Chaldon church. (A similar procession takes this route with the body of Hester Craddock in Alyse Gregory's novel of that name.) His grave stands, erect, close to the churchyard gate. On it are carved the words, surely written by Llewelyn, 'In Memory of Walter Franzen of New York City who met his death Falling in full Sunshine From a cliff at West Bottom May 26 1927 aged 34. The glory of young men is their strength and the beauty of old men is the grey head'. Another, more transient memorial was left on the cliffs where his towel had been discovered - 'some chalk stones in the shape of a cross', as Katie recorded in her journal.

This cross could double as a memorial to the inshore fishermen whose living was soon to dwindle until now when only a few lobster-pots remain. Harry Miller was the last of the Ringstead fishermen. He died in 1970, at the age of eighty, and is buried in the seaside graveyard of the little wooden church of St. Catherine-by-the-sea, Holworth, where he was churchwarden. The church was built in 1926. For some forty years before its building, services were held in a room of nearby Holworth House, and a token tithe of prawns given to the ecclesiastical parish of Milton as, in medieval times, Holworth had supplied Milton Abbey with 'salt-water fish'. It is thus an apt setting for a fisherman. Harry Miller's epitaph reads, 'A Great Friend to All'.

Harry Miller's home village of Ringstead was one of the places Llewelyn loved. 'Truly it was a legendary sea valley,' he wrote in *A Baker's Dozen*, 'with its stiles built of old oars, with woods gay with butterfly orchids, and with every field thick-spangled with elphin flowers'.

Here sea and coastline intermingle.

In Dorset, the grass is often mown down to the salt sea's edge, green against blue, so that on late mackerel evenings, fishermen laying lobster-pots on subaqueous rocky beds far out to sea can still smell the land of that lovely county, with its leafy lanes, its pink-campion woods, with its close-set twilight gardens, and its wide-stretching acres of fast drying prostrate herbs.

69. Gamel Woolsey and Llewelyn Powys.

Ringstead was for some time especially dear to Llewelyn because it sheltered 'the little poetess', Gamel Woolsey. Llewelyn had first met Gamel in New York in the winter of 1927 - 8, whilst he was acting as visiting critic for the *New York Herald Tribune*. Llewelyn and Alyse had once again taken rooms in Patchin Place, close to John Cowper Powys and his companion, Phyllis Playter. Below them lived Gamel Woolsey and her husband Rex Hunter, who were then in the process of separation.

171

Elizabeth Gammell Woolsey was born in South Carolina into an eminent family whose members included Sarah Chauncey Woolsey (better known as Susan Coolidge, author of *What Katy Did* and its sequels) and Gamel's half-brother, John M. Woolsey, the American judge who ruled that *Ulysses* was not obscene. Gamel was a strangely beautiful woman, with grey eyes, slanting and dreamy, set in a melancholy face. Like Llewelyn she suffered from tuberculosis, having had part of a lung removed in 1915. With Llewelyn too she shared a love for romantic literature, and both cherished fond recollections of childhood. Realising that Llewelyn was attracted to this enchanted woman, Alyse (by her own account) suggested that he should go to see her while she herself was visiting her parents in Norwalk. It was a moment of anger she must have afterwards regretted - by the time she returned, two days later, Llewelyn and Gamel were lovers. By the summer of 1928, Gamel was pregnant.

70. Gertrude Powys woodcut for 'Unicorn Legends' in Llewelyn Powys's collection of essays *Earth Memories*, 1934.

It was hardly the first occasion on which Llewelyn had been unfaithful to his wife - not that he would have regarded his behaviour in such a light. Alyse and he had agreed to place no restraints on one another's sexual freedom. It was not even the first occasion another woman was intent on bearing his child. Betty Marsh, wife of the painter, Reginald Marsh, had followed Powys from America (and taken a cottage at Ringstead) for that purpose in 1925. Alyse later claimed that when she had met him, Llewelyn had shown no interest in children (and she was, in any case, rather old to have a child) but her failure, as she saw it, saddened her. Yet Gamel also proved unable to bear a child. She had been pregnant when she married Rex Hunter; that pregnancy was terminated because of the delicate state of her health. The loss of Llewelyn's child, said to have been caused by an accident in a taxi, was the first of several miscarriages.

When in May 1929 Llewelyn and Alyse returned to England from an extended stay in Palestine, Naples, and Anacapri, Gamel followed them over, hoping to become pregnant again. On his travels, Llewelyn had been seriously ill with tuberculosis and kidney stone, and in her journals Alyse's anxieties concentrate on his precarious physical condition. Whilst away they received the news both of Gamel's pregnancy and of its unexpected ending.

Arriving in Dorset, Gamel lodged with the Toms, a fishing family in Ringstead. Alyse was apprehensive about her visit, but wrote on August 3rd, with relieved surprise, that the summer had been a happy one and that she had learned to love and appreciate Gamel. In this pleasantly peaceful summer, Gamel once again became pregnant, but her second pregnancy was to be even shorter than her first. She began to show signs of consumption, an abortion was advised, and in mid-August Llewelyn and Alyse accompanied her to a London nursing home. Llewelyn was deeply distressed by Gamel's suffering, and by the loss of his child.

Her convalescence over, Gamel moved to Mrs Wallis's cottage in Chaldon, considerably further from the White Nose, thus necessitating longer visits by Llewelyn, while making evening calls more difficult. Alyse did not interfere, although she noted with pain how Gamel was 'making herself more and more essential to L.'s life, learning his little ways that I know as I know my own pulse beats, immolating herself to please him, mending his clothes, correcting his manuscripts, studying the things that interest him . . .' The role of handmaiden suited Gamel, and was a less dangerous one than that of mistress. The abortion had changed the course of the affair, leaving Alyse, as she saw it, outside and excluded.

Terrified of losing Llewelyn, Alyse tried to live her life uncomplainingly apart; she contemplated suicide, made scrupulous record of her anguished feelings. In *Hester Craddock* published in 1931, Hester commits suicide by jumping off the 'Black Nore' in an attempt to secure her sister's happiness with the man they both love. As a proud, independent woman, Alyse seldom failed in her loyal support of her husband, indeed her self-torture reached limits that most other women would have found intolerable. Gamel was younger and, she thought, more beautiful than she, 'She will have his child', Alyse wrote, 'she is a poet'. She even suspected that Gamel was a better writer. Gamel's autobiographical novel, *One Way of Love*, suppressed by Gollancz in 1930 at proof stage because of the explicit nature of the descriptions of love-making, suggests that she had been initiated into that art by her husband, Rex Hunter. Her languid sexuality, her elusiveness and apparent vulnerability, her curious passivity, drew many men to her (including, in later years, Bertrand Russell). In a rare moment of open

71. Aylse Gregory outside the coastguard cottages.

jealousy, Alyse wrote of a visit they made to see her in 1931: 'Gamel was in bed. She was pale with that Asiatic look she sometimes has that suggests a knowledge of the secret arts of love. L. could hardly bear to look at her'. If she ever showed her feelings, Alyse noted, Llewelyn would reproach her.

He, too, was unhappy. When with one woman, he worried about the other. His demands on both were unremitting - on the approving consent of the one and the willingness of the other to bear his child - which, in fact, in the wake of her previous experiences, Gamel was increasingly reluctant to do. Llewelyn's thoughts seem to have been mainly with Gamel, yet when things went wrong he turned to Alyse for comfort. His letters show the intensity of his love for Gamel, and his desire to share not only her life but the land of her poems, a magical middle kingdom where the unicorn roamed free. This unicorn treads its way delicately through Gamel's early poems. In *One Way of Love*, a magazine editor tells the heroine, 'How dare you talk about unicorns? There ought to be a closed season on unicorns'. The reader can only agree. Yet they are undoubtedly better handled in her poems than they become when Llewelyn takes the reins. In his letters to Gamel after the lovers' separation the unicorn becomes a milky-white frequenter of his dreams, a sweeter, weaker creature than Gamel's.

The letters, quickened by fear of losing both Gamel and his chance of having a child, recall in loving detail their life together in the Chaldon landscape. 'I had thought of being with you in that spinney below the secret garden the winter morning when we saw the last pink campions, the other side of the stile the top bar of which is an oak. I wonder whether you remember, and remember how we kissed each other standing on the bare patch of grassless ground on the other side of the wire where the tall bushes grow'. Such precise detail is important to Powys: place and person are tangled together like ivy in his memories. They had roamed together over some of the places most dear to him, like the White Nose, Ringstead, Osmington and Chaldon. Gamel had become the spirit of these places, and they reminded him when left alone most painfully of her.

The other district most beloved by Llewelyn, the Montacute of his childhood, is the setting for his highly romantic novel, *Love and Death*. The events of the book occur in 1911, the year in which Llewelyn returned from his first stay in a Swiss sanatorium. This summer he always regarded as a golden one, lacking a single element for perfection - the love of a girl. In the novel this crucial void is filled by a Gamel-like creature called Dittany Stone. The hero is considerably younger than his creator and so is a more suitable match for his heroine (he is in fact even younger than Llewelyn was in 1911). In *Love and Death* Dittany Stone deserts the hero to marry his rival, after which she dies. In reality, in 1931, Gamel Woolsey married another man, and was to survive the experience for thirty-seven years.

Llewelyn's rival, as he saw it, was the writer Gerald Brenan. He had come to Chaldon in 1930 on the recommendation (yet again) of Stephen Tomlin, and almost the first person he saw on arrival was a young woman whom he took to be Katie Powys, wandering dreamily up the hill looking for flints. He was further intrigued to discover that she had lived for a year in the village without bothering to unpack her suitcase.

Brenan's account of the affair in *Personal Record*, a part of his autobiography, is written with considerable hindsight and an attempt at objectivity. The impressions left by the other three are more immediate, with Alyse's journal, a compelling document, coming closest of all. Gamel alone remains elusive. In her poem 'Middle Earth' she describes her own, langorous state of mind.

> On middle earth the days go by
> Silently and steadily;
> It is not heaven, it is not hell,
> But for the living does as well . . .
>
> With secret pain, with open mirth,
> I go my way on middle earth.

When Gerald Brenan appeared in Chaldon, Gamel was already preparing to abandon her affair with Llewelyn. It was painful for all concerned, she no longer wanted to risk having a child, and she was becoming increasingly attached to her fellow American, Alyse. (By the time of Llewelyn's death she seems, as can happen in a *ménage à trois*, to have become fonder of Alyse than of her former lover.) Brenan says that when he met her she was thinking of returning to America, and there is no reason to doubt this statement.

Brenan had come to Chaldon to work on a novel. He had, in November 1928, found himself at the end of a protracted love affair with Dora Carrington, wife of Ralph Partridge and devoted friend of Lytton Strachey. Now he was looking for a wife. As well as wishing for a less complicated relationship, he also needed a mother for his natural daughter. He had promised the child's Spanish mother than he would take full responsibility for his daughter when she became two years old. He soon decided that Gamel Woolsey was the woman he needed and so, as her departure seemed imminent, he asked her to marry him. Gamel had made no mention of her own love affair, and Gerald had no inkling of it. He had met Llewelyn and at once saw that he was in love with Gamel, and that Alyse was in despair about it. But to Brenan, Llewelyn Powys seemed 'so worn and racked by age and sickness'

72. Ray Garnett's dust-jacket design, 1931.

that it did not occur to him that the love might be returned. Brenan's description of Powys in *Personal Record* gives some indication of his dry reservations about a man whose character was so alien to his own.

Except for Willie, who farmed in Kenya, Llewelyn was the youngest of the six Powys brothers and he had always been a bit spoiled by his family. His appearance was striking: with his deeply furrowed cheeks and grey dishevelled beard and hair he suggested a preacher in some new-fangled religion, while his long cape and broad-brimmed hat bore out this impression. But he looked gay rather than solemn and in the button-hole of his heavy country tweeds he liked to wear a bright flower. Those who met him for the first time were usually captured by his charm, although this could sometimes be a little too mellifluous because he was given to propitiating anyone with whom he did not feel completely at ease. Underneath this there lay an obviously attractive personality, open and spontaneous and endowed with a tremendous zest for life . . .

This was the man with whom Gamel had been in love. When at last she gave Gerald a fuller account of the affair, Gamel (whose habit it was to avoid unpleasant subjects) said that it was all over and agreed to marry Gerald. Brenan suspected that she was using him as an escape from an intolerable situation, but this she denied, insisting that she was no longer in love with Powys.

After Gamel broke the news of her impending marriage to a distraught Llewelyn, he and Alyse left for London, going from there straight to America. Seeing the desperate state of her health after this distressing scene, Gertrude Powys suggested that Gamel should spend a night at Chydyok. Brenan called the next morning to discover that Gamel had suffered a slight haemorrhage and that she was once again remote and inaccessible, distanced (as he later realised) by guilt. A cosmic dimension was added to the situation when Gertrude explained to a bewildered Brenan that the love which bound Gamel to Llewelyn 'transcended all other loves. It had something supernatural about it which meant that nothing could ever quench it, not even the grave'. With Brenan's help, Gertrude went on, Gamel would recover. 'All would be well and this unseverable link would in due course be restored to what it had been before. It also seemed that the moon played some part in this sacred affinity, since vows had been solemnly made to it which had cemented it'.

Gertrude was not much given to such lunar fancies and they reveal, one must suppose, the strength of her desire to defend her brother. Llewelyn must be protected at all costs. (She had already reassured Alyse that she did not think Llewelyn would leave her for Gamel, as Alyse had given him the freedom to do.)

Separated from his lover, Llewelyn began to write the letters recalling his days with her amidst the cliffs and woods by the White Nose which prefigured his novel *Love and Death*. Gamel's responses, in which passionate lover soon becomes firm friend, are wise and careful of tone, thoughtful always for Alyse. In May 1931 Gerald Brenan and Gamel Woolsey went through a private wedding ceremony in Rome - Gamel was never actually divorced from Rex Hunter - and on their return to England set up house in Weld Cottage, East Lulworth. Llewelyn and Alyse were already back at White Nose where all four gathered on June 14th for afternoon tea. 'And so we sat', Alyse wrote, 'four puppets in this immemorial drama, spreading our toast with butter, while suspicion and fear and hope and anxiety peered from underneath . . . I felt pity for all of us, who could so strangely injure each other, four people so sensitive and well-meaning'.

Gerald Brenan and Alyse Gregory liked and respected one another being, brought rapidly to a polite understanding by their mutually excluded positions. Llewelyn, Gerald wrote, 'with the tears streaming down his cheeks' had begged him not to separate the lovers. Brenan, affected by his evident misery, and with acute memories of his own experience with Carrington, agreed to let his wife and Llewelyn meet. He was aware that this arrangement was likely to damage his marriage, but believed that 'Love had its claims that must be respected'. This belief was to cost him dearly, for it impaired his marriage from its very beginning - though perhaps in any case Gamel never loved Gerald. She needed a protector, she needed peace, she needed a way out. Their union, as reported in Brenan's books and Woolsey's letters, was low-key and civilised. Gamel's later feelings about it seemed to emerge in a poem like 'Picnicking at Ashdown'.

> We came too late, Oh, centuries too late.
> The wide stair echoed to a lonely tread.
> And stiff silks rustled by the broken gate . . .
>
> Where is the life we might have lived?

For his part, Llewelyn found Gerald's rational generosity, although he undoubtedly benefited from it, somewhat chilling. Brenan's letters, he once observed to Alyse, 'sometimes give you the feeling of being placed in the very outer circumference of his life where you hang like a jackdaw on a hazel stick with all your tail feathers to be examined with a cold dispassionate philosopher's eye'.

For his part too, Llewelyn continued to hope that Gamel would return to him - but, although he would not see it, the affair was virtually over.

Llewelyn never forgot Gamel, while Alyse, who had suffered and sacrificed herself for her husband, managed to survive the experience only by achieving a greater detachment from him. *King Log & Lady Lea* (1929), her story of a man in love with two women, presents a curiously dispassionate portrait of Llewelyn. Vain and weak, he becomes 'a mere empty figure' set up between the women. Humiliated by them, he is finally killed by a car. In this novel, Alyse takes her literary revenge. Yet in the next few years they shared moments of great happiness, made the more poignant because for much of the time Llewelyn was dangerously ill.

73. Chydyok from the south.

In November 1931 Llewelyn and Alyse moved down from White Nose to the smaller half of Chydyok Farm, next door to Gertrude and Katie. The cottage was rented, rent was paid annually on Michaelmas Day. The brick and flint building, slate-roofed, lies in a hollow of the hills, midway between village and sea. It was erected in 1900 on the site of a smaller dwelling, known as Vicarage Down Buildings (which had a pond in its enclosure). The builders of the new farm house came from Preston, a village six miles distant, and would walk along the cliffs to work and back again. Chydyok was probably never used as a farm, being even then at too remote a distance from other buildings. It was occupied by a gamekeeper and a family of carters and was originally called 'Chideock Farm' because the Welds, in addition to the lands they held around Chaldon, had estates (among other places) at Chideock near Bridport - where, incidentally, they built a second Catholic church. Llewelyn, discovering that the post was often delivered to the wrong Chideock, changed the spelling of the name to Chydyok, despite a warning from his brother Bertie not to 'monkey' with placenames.

Llewelyn brought down his shelter from the White Nose, erecting it first on the sheltered northern side of the Round Pound, a prehistoric cattle enclosure, now overgrown with nettles, gorse and rusty dock, about half a mile from the house. When he became chronically ill, it was removed to the top of the garden, and in the garden a restored shelter still stands. On the base are inscribed the words, 'Long life 0 sun June 1934'. Here he spent most of his time, being cared for by Alyse and Gertrude. Alyse, whose ambitions had not included housekeeping, was slow and inefficient at the daily tasks expected of her, but she took on the full burden of work. Katie's journal for 1927 observes of Alyse that 'It's generally she that takes the weight and responsibility of all' and this was increasingly the case. Llewelyn's health was a constant worry, and in 1933 he was so close to death that he sought permission from Herbert Weld to be buried (knees to chin, like an old warrior) on the cliffs.

There were, fortunately, some vital links with the village. Milk came from the farm, William Treviss walked up to do the gardening. The Chaldon bee-keeper and carpenter, Walter Miller (brother of Harry), converted the loft for Llewelyn and made the steps leading to it (the boat-like loft became Alyse's sitting-room). The plans for this were drawn up by the architect Bertie to Llewelyn's specific instructions. The garden was laid out in terraces and a pond dug by the front door, engraved with the words 'Good Hope lies at the bottom'. Walter Miller was an invaluable help in the improvements, he was a good craftsman, and could turn his hand to anything, using for his carpentry any scrap of wood that came to hand. He carved a corner cupboard out of a section of the village footbridge, for instance, and the frame for the applique picture in Chaldon church was made by him from teak driftwood. From village stories, his bee-keeping seems to have been a more unruly occupation. Jim Pitman's father, Isaac, was stung on his bald head in Walter's garden, while the harvest festival service of 1937 had in addition to its decorations of marrows, corn and Michaelmas daisies, a humming cloud of escaped bees.

From his sickbed, Llewelyn corresponded with Walter and introduced Miller's young son, Rowland, to subjects like archaeology and history. Llewelyn had a concerned interest in the villagers, to whom he behaved like an old-fashioned squire, friendly and bountiful. In 1929 he wrote letters on behalf of the two Ringstead fishermen whose summer livelihood was threatened by the arrival of an Admiralty surveying boat. One of his last acts before he died in exile in Switzerland was to draw up a list of gifts for the village children, to be sent from a London store.

74. Walter Miller, village carpenter.

A daily-anticipated event must have been the arrival of the post. Mr K. R. Bakes, whose postman father collected the mail in Chaldon, has provided, in tribute to his memory, an account of S. G. Bakes's work. Chaldon was (and is) serviced by the G.P.O. from Dorchester. Before 1920 some of the mail was transported by bike as far as Winfrith and then on to Chaldon. Mary Jane Legg at Chaldon was the last stopping-point, the others being Broadmayne, Warmwell, Owermoigne and Winfrith. 'Having reached Chaldon' writes Mr Bakes, 'a break of some two hours was taken before commencing the return journey to Dorchester. Part of this time was for the postman to have his official break, usually half-an-hour, and a further hour was allowed for the cleaning of the Mail Van'. On the return journey, mail was collected from post-offices and boxes.

Security was important as the mail often contained money, valuables and important documents. Newspapers were daily delivered and sometimes medicines, in bulky glass bottles. Chaldon Post Office opened in 1894 when the post-mistress was Louisa Pitman. From 1904 the post-mistress was Mary Jane Legg, 'Grannie' Legg as she was later affectionately known. There she was, there she stayed, at the centre of village life until the beginning of the Second World War when she retired as, growing increasingly blind, she could not abide the thought of ration books and the accompanying forms. She was succeeded by Mrs House, who ran the post office from the neighbouring detached building, then known as 'Sandhurst'. Hers was a post office only, without a shop, though she continued to sell cod-liver oil, orange juice, and powdered milk for babies.

Despite this move, the postwoman remained the same. She was Mrs Lucas, wife of Billy - and Mrs Lucas it was who carried the post to Chydyok. She leaves an impression of great energy. Up the hills she strode with her stick, along 'Bloater Lane' (as Chydyok Road was then known) over Chalky Knap and down the track which curves like a segment of silvery-white moon - a laborious journey sometimes made the longer by detours to avoid the cattle of which she was terrified. Llewelyn's nephew, Peter Powys Grey, remembered her well. He recalled the 'great wen on her forehead and the wisdom in her eye, red-trimmed "GR" postmistress cap on her head and the mistiness all over her coat, bursting into Chydyok with fine gossip and the best of kippers, her Dorset-talk thick and embracing'. The Chydyok post especially must have been heavy with parcels of books, but Mrs Lucas went on delivering for years, eventually becoming the oldest postwoman in Dorset and the second oldest in the country. She received an imperial service medal for her work. In addition, she did the cleaning for Gertrude and Katie. On the other side of the house, the cleaning was done by the beautiful Lil Jacobs (sister of Alice Hewlett) and later by Mrs Treviss. Milk was delivered to outlying houses by various school children - Rowland Miller, for instance, remembers delivering at Rat's Barn.

Llewelyn, generous to a fault, would offer hospitality to his callers. He pressed cans of beer on eleven-year-old Ken Blandamer, as well as the books he liked all the village people to have. Whilst at Chydyok, he worked on despite his illness. In 1933 he was writing *Love and Death*, but found himself more often composing 'very short and utterly "perfect" articles for the *Dorset*

Echo' which he much enjoyed doing, as he explained to Rivers Pollock: 'I have a mania for doing this. I like the idea of giving to the Dorset labourers and shepherds and furze cutters the *very best writing* and it thrills me when I hear of some essay being discussed in a Dorset tavern'.

Some of the *Dorset Essays* are amongst his best work, though others are coloured by his consciousness of himself as a West Country figure - which in fact he did become, as the national publicity given to the libel case showed. He paid tribute to that other greater and more famous West Country figure, Thomas Hardy, the necessary pioneer of the idea of Wessex, an entity with Dorset at its heart. Powys had known the older writer personally - Hardy had called on his bicycle at Montacute Vicarage, and Llewelyn had visited Max Gate. In *Skin for Skin*, Llewelyn and Theodore are shown walking homeward together past Max Gate on Christmas Eve. Inside, as Llewelyn imagines, is the renowned old figure, still alive in his Dorset world. *Thirteen Worthies*, of which Hardy is (appropriately enough) the thirteenth and last, is dedicated to the man 'whose footfalls still, by the Grace of God, indent the turnpike roads, the honeysuckle lanes, the flinty ewe-cropped downs of the ancient county of Dorset'.

The included worthies are not all Dorset men, but have been chosen from amongst the men from whom Powys feels a literary descent, men like Chaucer, for example, who was 'blessed with a lust for existence as unflagging as it was unequalled', or Thomas Culpeper whose 'extraordinary and rambling writings . . . reveal the closest knowledge and observation of nature'. As in a similar collection, *Rats in the Sacristy*, he is mainly selecting writers who endorse his own beliefs. He shows little interest in argument or dialogue about his theories.

In his *Book of Days* he traces the origins of his philosophy even further back: to the ancient sun-worshippers, adopting the Egyptian ankh as his symbol. There is one 'glorious and apparent God' acknowledged by him in *Impassioned Clay* and that is the 'unvanquished and visible sun'. Llewelyn believed that each human being should love his life, for which the sun is the source, enjoying every moment of it to the full. Of earthly experiences, love is the greatest: 'Mutual desire is its own justification at all times and in all places'. Love must be accepted wherever we can find it, since life is short and non-returning.

Powys is highly critical of Christianity because, he claims, it underestimates the value of sexual love and attempts to curb it as a force. Such an attitude, he argues in *Glory of Life*, a book which at the time of its publication created much excitement - and disapproval - does not make him unreligious. 'The deepest religious mood', Powys maintains, 'is a religious mood that in no way depends upon belief in a God'. The proof of this lies less in the arguments than in the fervent power of the writing. In his first published work, *Confessions of Two Brothers* (1916), Llewelyn wrote, 'To be suddenly born, to suddenly acquire consciousness on the surface of this unsteady and amazing planet, that is a chance indeed to justify everything'. He kept to the end the sense of wonder, the child's ability to see the world ever anew, which infuses the best of his writing.

75. Llewelyn outside Chydok.   76. Ankh by Gertrude Powys.

In his scheme of things, death has a salty importance. 'For us the dread of death adds a tang and relish to life', he wrote in *Ebony and Ivory*. Death entered Llewelyn's life early. His sister Eleanor died of peritonitis at the age of thirteen, and eight-year-old Llewelyn was much affected by this event. In *Threnody*, an essay on Eleanor's death, Powys describes the conclusion drawn by himself as a young child witnessing his sister's unexpected disappearance: 'surely the secret of so sorry and insecure an existence must lie in detachment for he who would lose his heart to a life so beset with tragedy had best have a care for his wits'. Detachment is not a quality one

185

always associates with Llewelyn, and such a statement is at odds with his habitual whole-hearted approach to life. Detachment is a useful quality, though, in an essay like *Threnody*, or the essay on the drowning of Walter Franzen, 'A Grave in Dorset', or the lament for the sudden death of Albert Reginald Powys, where the quality of the writing is transformed by the writer's ability to distance himself from his subject.

Like his brother Theodore, Llewelyn gave much thought to death, including its more macabre aspects. A major difference between their attitudes is revealed by a conversation of about 1933 when Theodore asked his brother, '"If you could die this moment without pain, without knowledge that you were going to die, would you accept the opportunity?" Theodore said that he himself would accept with relief and gratitude, but Llewelyn vigorously declared that he would accept any future uncertainty rather than part with life'.

Human cruelty was another subject which preoccupied both Theodore and Llewelyn (and their brother John). Whilst in Kenya during the First World War, Llewelyn witnessed some pitiless cruelty. More than once in his essays he describes how he came across a group of Kikuyu children crucifying a hawk, and how he had to will himself to intervene. He was not afraid to analyse the extent to which he enjoyed the sight of such suffering and observed, 'How powerful a current in life is this particular blood-hot emotion'. In *Skin for Skin* he tells how he stood by as a stoat wrestled with a rabbit on the heath, while his companion Theodore threw stones at the struggling creatures to try and make an end. With Llewelyn it was not always so. Alyse wrote that he could not bear the sufferings of a rabbit in a gin, but where Theodore's cruel streak was confined to his fiction, Llewelyn's was more likely to spill over into real life. More importantly, though causing suffering to others was in his creed the major sin, in the pursuance of his love affair with Gamel Woolsey he was being cruel, however unwittingly, however unavoidably, to his wife. His simple philosophy of life was ill-adapted to the complexities of that affair.

Powys at all times tried to live out his life according to his own personal beliefs which, oft and grandly stated as they are, cannot be dismissed as mere empty words. Alyse wrote in her introduction to his *Letters* that she 'often pondered on his power of sustaining so many hours, so many years indeed, in his bed with so much gaiety and wisdom'. Happiness came naturally to Llewelyn. As a child he was remembered for his joyous dancing cry of 'Happy me! Happy me!' (as well as for the present he once hung on the Christmas tree labelled 'To Lulu from Lulu'). He was an attractive man with, in his youth, a halo of golden hair. (A chunk of this hair, wiry and vital, was used by Walter Miller when plastering Gertrude and Katie's porch. He had run out of the horse hair he used to make the plaster cling, so Llewelyn offered some of his own.)

Despite his many and serious illnesses, Powys continued to take risks with his health - to court death - in order to make use of every moment. His writings, in their instances of vibrant intensity, reveal how close he had sometimes come to that death which he both challenged and wished to avoid at all costs. His illness constantly reminded him of the brevity of life, and so did his surroundings. On the Dorset cliffs, at the White Nose and Chydyok, thousands of ages can be encompassed at a glance. There are earthworks like Wardstone Barrow on the highest point of the downs by Chydyok, or Bush Barrow, with its tangled crown of thorn. One of the flint circles at nearby Chainey Bottom was excavated in 1930 by a group who included Albert Powys, another brother fascinated with prehistory. Llewelyn's reflections, too, can be triggered by the forgotten fragments he sees, like the old clock weight in his Chydyok garden, the mere handling of which 'stirred the imagination'; the stump of the old cross on the village green, or (in 'Natural Worship') a derelict carriage in Lulworth Park.

Llewelyn had once bought a book entitled *How to Write* and, John Cowper Powys tells us, read and re-read the masters of prose for the same instructive purpose. He made careful use of dictionaries and reference books (although Alyse Gregory observed that he was apt to be 'irresponsible' and 'inaccurate' about small details) and took his studies seriously, consciously following the tradition of English essayists like William Hazlitt. Partly because the essays were mostly written for individual publication, he cites again and again the same examples. Examples of these examples, taken at random, include the comparison of a skull to a pot of bone, of the outline of a Swiss mountain to a recumbent Queen Victoria, the use of the country rhyme 'Apples be Ripe' and of John Cowper Powys's version of it, the anecdote of the churchyard cough - and most conspicuous of all, since he seldom mentions the visual arts, the references to Breughel's painting 'The Month of August'. His style is often rhetorically eloquent, and he possessed to the highest degree the family talent for self-dramatisation - 'Luluising' his family called it - which could sometimes degenerate into mere staginess. He had a fondness for mythologising the people he knew, beginning with his family: and not only Theodore received this treatment. In 'A Smuggler's Path' Llewelyn, whilst exploring the beach at Middle Bottom, finds a dead seagull from which he cuts off a wing 'to carry back as a gift to my sweet sea-gull sister'. Katie, the

77. One of Robert Gibbings' engravings for *Glory of Life*, 1934.

sister intended, was unlikely to have welcomed such a gift, even from her beloved Llewelyn. This essay caused some amusement even at the time. 'What a revolting present!' Sylvia Townsend Warner remarked to Theodore. 'Did he expect her to put it among her handkerchieves?'

Outside family and friends, Powys wrote essays on West Country heroes like the Duke of Monmouth, the Tolpuddle Martyrs, and Sidney Godolphin Osborne, Victorian champion of the Dorsetshire labourers. Nor do the Chaldon villagers entirely escape this treatment, Walter Miller for example, whose 'wise head' is able to identify the disinterred clock weight, or James Cobb, whose steady nature Llewelyn so much admired and celebrated.

Despite such lofty tendencies, Powys's knowledge of the Dorset places is intimate and detailed. He had travelled over the world from the deserts of Arizona to California and New York, to Israel, Africa and Switzerland, observantly appreciating many and different landscapes. But Dorset was where he belonged, and where his thoughts turned, from the most distant and dissimilar of scenes. Christmas in New York finds him remembering how 'at that very hour the lights from the cottage windows of East Chaldon were, I knew, shining out into the darkness, visible as far away as the steep downland sheep-track . . . ' In another section of *The Verdict of Bridlegoose*, Alyse's room in Patchin Place is likened to a fisherman's cottage on the Isle of Portland. Both are shelters from the outside storms, but Dorset is ever the dearer.

Llewelyn was, as his schoolmaster brother Littleton wrote, 'intensely alive to every person and thing around him' and no more alertly so than when he was on home territory. There he could sense the very ground beneath his feet. In his essay on 'St. Aldhelm's Head' he notices how 'As we pass from field to field we become more and more conscious that the tremendous stone foundations of the locality are only a little way below our shoe-leather'. His awareness was linked to his close knowledge of the district. In 'High Chaldon', an essay that describes how the herring gulls, white on green, settle on the hilly turf in wet weather, Powys truly remarks, 'I do not suppose there is an elder tree, thorn tree, holly tree, or gorse bush that is unknown to me in those fields'. His knowledge is as closely-mapped as his brother Theodore's, though where one is inclined to mud, the other preferred the stars. The depth of his knowledge emerges in some of the essays. 'In 'Bats Head', for example, he reveals how 'On afternoons of the wildest weather a man may rest here in tranquillity, some peculiarity in the structure of the cliff causing the rushing gales to cast themselves straight up from its sheer walls, so that the crest of the headland remains in absolute calm'.

There are moments of great beauty in his writing. In *The Twelve Months*, the section on September ends with a glowing, humming miniature of the early autumn season.

Every thorn hedge is now brushed with scarlet, so densely do the haws congregate. Holly berries that will be carried home bright as cocks' combs to adorn Christmas plum puddings are, though fully formed, as yet grass green. The matted ivy that hangs from the grange is in flower and the unbelievable number of peacock butterflies settled upon it suggest a damask pattern upon medieval tapestry. All day long there is a murmur of flies and gnats, their thin ephemeral trumpet voices giving place to an unnatural silence that falls upon wood and orchard as soon as the sun has gone down. This silence is deeper and more impressive than was ever experienced during the tremulous white nights of midsummer.

At other times he can achieve a mysteriously magical quality. In 'A Downland Burden' he recounts a walk he once made over from Lodmoor with a parcel of six herrings which he intended to deliver to Theodore at dawn. Light is beginning to break as he reaches West Chaldon, where he sees a candle burning in a cottage window, a scene which suggests to him the 'cockroach wintry warm-retaining early morning kitchens'. On his journey he had stopped, once, in the centre of Poxwell stone circle. Here he arranged his herrings in a row, where they lay enclosed, 'their plump sides in the moonlight more glittering than the frost'.

Llewelyn died in Switzerland on December 2, 1939, three years to the day after leaving Dorset for the last time. Tuberculosis did not finally kill him, he died of a stomach ulcer. Alyse was with him to the end.

Alyse Gregory returned to England and stayed on at Chydyok until 1957, gradually learning to live without Llewelyn. In her journal there are bitter moments. In January 1942 she wrote, 'I know I often felt imprisoned with L., pulled into his thoughts, crushed by his illnesses, destroyed by his infidelities, subsisting on anxiety for my daily diet, never owning my own soul'. Memories of love, though, were usually stronger. In April 1943 she wrote, 'People always say that time heals our wounds and gradually obliterates the sorrow we feel over the death of someone we love. I have not found this true. Memories come as piercingly to me as ever'.

Left alone, Alyse had early made a resolution 'not to obtrude my own feelings anywhere, to try only to reach into others' thoughts, to expect nothing in the way of understanding, to be subtle in hiding my pain, to throw my interest into every little thing I see'. She listened to music, read and re-read the works of Proust, offered wise and tolerant advice to those around her - particularly Valentine Ackland, whom she both encouraged and consoled.

Around her, life went on, and her journal records snatches of it. On each New Year's Eve the bells of Lulworth and Chaldon Herring could be heard (a sound beloved by Llewelyn). During the invasion scare of 1940 Curtie Legg, aged sixteen, guarded the cliffs all night - with a truncheon. In 1946 there was a sports day when the inn was full of tipsy revellers and fireworks exploded over the Five Marys. Twelve carol singers appeared at Christmas 1949. 'They came up in the mist led by their stalwart fiddler, their lights flashing in the darkness like fireflies'.

Incidents like this flicker in the dimness of Alyse's later life. There were visits, of course, and visitors, but as Alyse wrote to Valentine Ackland in 1947, for the most part she lived alone 'with cows, seagulls, flints, and my own unreliable thoughts'.

After the war Llewelyn's ashes were brought back from Switzerland. On September 6th, 1947, Alyse went to Portland with her brother-in-law, Littleton, Gertrude and Betty Muntz to choose a memorial stone. They went 'Up, up, up over roads powdered with dazzling white stone dust . . . into the veritable world of nothing but stone - stones of gigantic size piled one upon the other as far as the eye could see, stones tumbled about in every direction.'

On September 28, Gertrude, Katie and Alyse buried the ashes on the cliff 'in the place dug by Mr Treviss, 3 feet deep in chalk'. There, on October 3rd, the stone was lowered into place, the head quarry man remarking, 'It will last a thousand years, it will last forever'. On it Elizabeth Muntz carved the words Llewelyn had chosen for his epitaph:

The living The living He shall praise thee

And, lichened now, the stone still stands amidst the grass at the field's edge. It has become, as Llewelyn would have wished it, part of the Chaldon landscape.

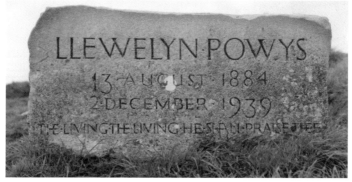

78. Llewelyn's memorial stone on the Dorset clifftop.

79. Shell sculpture by Peter Randall-Page, 1985/86, part of Common Ground's New Milestones project, on the cliffs above Chaldon.

Afterword

'Life do get too vast.'   Billy Lucas.

The name Chaldon can mean 'a place of calves' or more tellingly, 'a place of shelter'. In the garden of the manor house the roses bloom on soil only inches deep, sheltered as they are from the worst of the weather by the stony, bony hills. The hills' protection makes Chaldon lullingly peaceful and secure, but this is deceptive. The village's calm has a flinty edge, roughened as it has been by centuries of hard labour and poor living. The hills are bowed by poverty and age.

Poverty was an aspect of village life which not even the hastiest, most blinkered of visitors could fail to notice. The tied and swarming cottages bred lives which were often narrow and suspicious, though surprisingly tolerant of the behaviour of the artistic incomers, to whom the unwritten laws of village life seem seldom to have been applied. There was as well a gossipy vitality, an unaffected kindliness and hospitality which older people in Chaldon, reflecting on the shining days of their youth, say has now been lost, as the old patterns of family and friends die away, to be only partially replaced. Noticeably lost, and unmourned, is the worst of the need.

The years, as well as poverty, wear down the hills, and an awareness of a distant past, of prehistory, is a constant in the village. The past lies close to the surface, and can be easily, almost casually destroyed by tractor or running deer, or thrown into sudden prominence by the angled rays of the winter's sun. Chaldon is full of ghostly echoes which the ear strains to catch, echoes from the dreams of childhood, or reaching back way beyond any private memory. In the village the past is ever-present, like the poverty which even Theodore Powys found unholy; like the recurring sense of death. The dancing stones in the churchyard mark time for bones.

This is the atmosphere, seasoned by the sea's salt tang, which pervades the books of the writers who worked in the village. If there is a 'school of Chaldon' then it is the landscape - sometimes as examined by T. F. Powys - which orders it. Much fascinating work was produced here, some of it of a very high quality, like *Mr Weston's Good Wine*, a number of Llewelyn Powys's Dorset essays and of Sylvia Townsend Warner's poems and stories.

The Chaldon landscape is still compelling a response. On the cliffs close by Llewelyn's memorial are three stone niches containing whorled sculptures of snails, recently installed. The snails are carved of Purbeck marble, not a true marble in fact, but a blue limestone. Thus they are re-creations from thousands of tiny fossilised snails, exotic, extinct - and local. They roundly recall the shapes of winding valley and hill.

The outline of the place has changed but little in the last hundred years. Old postcards are instantly identifiable. The harsh splendour of the valley remains, but is under threat, like so much of the English countryside in these mean and greedy times. The threats are familiar: ill-advised new buildings, the conversion of old ones to holiday cottages, and the slick menace of oil - though this latter threat is hardly new. The D'Arcy Exploration Company drilled Chaldon Down for oil in 1938, a process interrupted by the outbreak of war. In 1954 there was a proposal to drill for oil on West Chaldon Farm: a scheme which would have required a new road to service it. In the 1990s, Amoco drilled in West Chaldon, without success. (The fact that the coast above Chaldon is now part of a World Heritage Site may offer some protection from futher exploitation.)

So far the village remains fragilely intact, recognisable for what it always has been, a humble and isolated agricultural settlement. Or else, glimpsed at twilight or in uneasy weather, as unexpectedly beautiful, untamed and sinister as an owl.

80. Shell sculpture by Peter Randall-Page.

Bibliography

Introduction
Kenneth Hopkins, *The Powys Brothers*, Warren House, Norfolk, 1972
John Hutchins, *History of Dorset* Vol.1, 3rd edn., London, 1861
Llewelyn Powys, *Skin for Skin*, Cape, 1926
Victoria History of the County of Dorset Vol.II, Archibald Constable, 1908
Dorset Record Office, Proposal to build a light railway between Lulworth and Osmington, 1896, 1899

1. *The Five Marys*
I. *Published Sources*
Joan Berkeley, *Lulworth and the Welds*, Blackmore Press, 1971
Countess de Boigne, *Memoirs* (Vols.I & II), 1820 - 1830, Heinemann, 1907 & 1908
Madame de Boigne, *Mémoires* (Vol.II), Mercure de France, 1971
Vicomte François René de Chateaubriand, Mémoires d'Outre-Tombe (Vols.III & IV), Paris 1949 - 50
Dorset County Chronicle, Aug.-Oct. 1830
Mary Frampton, *Journals*, 1779-1846, (ed. Mundy), Sampson Low, 1885
Duchess de Gontaut, *Memoirs* (Vol. II), Chatto & Windus, 1894
Ronald Good, *Lost Villages of Dorset*, Dovecote Press, 1979
Ronald Good, *The Old Roads of Dorset*, Bournemouth, 1966
L. V. Grinsell, *Dorset Barrows*, Dorset Natural History & Archaeological Society, 1959
Florence Emily Hardy, *The Life of Thomas Hardy*, Macmillan, 1962
Thomas Hardy, *Wessex Tales*, Macmillan, 1912
M. F. Heathcote, *Lulworth and its Neighbourhood*, Winchester, 1906
T. E. B. Howarth, *Citizen-King*, Eyre & Spottiswood, 1961
John Hutchins, *History of Dorset* (Vol. I), 3rd ed., London 1861
A. L. Imbert de Saint-Armand, *La Cour de Charles X*, Paris, 1892
John & Muriel Lough, *An Introduction to 19th Century France*, Longman, 1978
Barry M. Marsden, *The Early Barrow Diggers*, Shire, 1974
Nikolaus Pevsner, *Dorset*, Penguin, 1972
Poole & Bournemouth Herald, Aug.-Oct. 1830

Llewelyn Powys, *Dorset Essays*, Redcliffe Press, 1983
Liewelyn Powys, *Skin for Skin*, Cape, 1926
P. A. Rahtz, 'Holworth Medieval Village Excavation 1958', *Proceedings of the Dorset Natural History & Archaeological Society* (Vol. 81), 1959
Royal Commission on Historical Monuments, *Dorset* (Vol.II, Pts.I & III), 1970
Friedrich Sieburg, *Chateaubriand*, Allen & Unwin, 1961
Christopher Taylor, *Dorset*, Hodder & Stoughton, 1970
Charles Warne, *Celtic Tumuli of Dorset*, 1866

II *Unpublished Sources*
Dorset Record Office, Weld Estate Papers

2 *Theodore Powys at Beth Car*
I *Published Sources*
Valentine Ackland, *For Sylvia*, Chatto & Windus, 1985
William Barnes, *A Glossary of the Dorset Dialect*, Toucan Press, 1970
Glen Cavaliero, *The Rural Tradition in the English Novel*, Macmillan, 1977*
A Chatto & Windus Miscellany, 1928
The Countryman (Vol.2, No.1), 1928
The Countryman (Vol.4, No.1), 1930
The Countryman October 1934.
Department of the Environment, *List of Buildings of Special Architectural or Historic Interest, District of Purbeck, Dorset*, 1984
David Garnett (ed.), *Carrington*, Cape, 1970*
David Garnett, *The Familiar Faces*, Chatto & Windus, 1962
Richard Perceval Graves, *The Brothers Powys*, Routledge, 1983
Helen Hardy, 'By Carrier to Dorchester', *The Countryman*, Autumn 1975
Thomas Hardy, *Tess of the d'Urbervilles*, 1891*
R. F. Harrod, *The Life of John Maynard Keynes*, Macmillan, 1951
Belinda Humfrey (ed.), *Recollections of the Powys Brothers*, Peter Owen, 1980
Rosemary Manning, 'Theodore, the Great Neglected', *Dorset*, No. 45, 1975
Liam O'Flaherty, *Shame the Devil*, Grayson, 1934
Nikolaus Pevsner, *Dorset*, Penguin, 1972
Michel Pouillard, 'T. F. Powys and the Theatre', *Powys Review* 5, 1979
Michel Poulliard, 'Woman and Women in T. F. Powys's Novels', *Powys Review* 12, 1983
Count Potocki of Montalk, *Dogs' Eggs* (Part 1), Mélissa Press, 1968
John Cowper Powys, *Autobiography*, Macdonald, 1967
John Cowper Powys, *Letters to his Brother Llewelyn* (Vols.I & II), Village Press, 1975
John Cowper Powys, *Letters to Louis Wilkinson, 1935-1956*, Macdonald, 1958
Llewelyn Powys, 'Conversations with Theodore', *Powys Review* 4, 1978/79
Littleton Powys, 'The Powys Family', pamphlet issued by *Western Gazette*, 1953
Theodore Francis Powys, *Black Bryony*, Chatto & Windus, 1923

Theodore Francis Powys, *Bottle's Path*, Chatto & Windus, 1946

Theodore Francis Powys, *Innocent Birds*, Chatto & Windus, 1926*

Theodore Francis Powys, *An Interpretation of Genesis*, privately printed, 1907

Theodore Francis Powys, *Kindness in a Corner*, Chatto & Windus, 1930*

Theodore Francis Powys, *The Left Leg*, Chatto & Windus, 1923

Theodore Francis Powys, *Mark Only*, Chatto & Windus, 1924

Theodore Francis Powys, *Mr Tasker's Gods*, Chatto & Windus, 1925*

Theodore Francis Powys, *Mr Weston's Good Wine*, Chatto & Windus, 1927*

Theodore Francis Powys, *Mockery Gap*, Chatto & Windus, 1925*

Theodore Francis Powys, 'The Child Queen', *Powys Newsletter* 1, 1970

Theodore Francis Powys, *Soliloquies of a Hermit*, Andrew Melrose, 1918

Theodore Francis Powys, *Unclay*, Chatto & Windus, 1931*

Peter Riley, *A Bibliography of T. F. Powys*, R. A. Brimmell, Hastings, 1967

Theodora Scutt, 'Theodore Powys, 1934-1953', *Powys Review* 9, 1981/2

Theodora Scutt, 'Theodore Powys, 1934-1953' (continuation), *Powys Review* 10, 1982

Dylan Thomas, *Quite Early One Morning,* Dent, 1954

R. H. Ward, *The Powys Brothers*, Bodley Head, 1935

Sylvia Townsend Warner, *Collected Poems* (ed. with an introduction by Claire Harman), Carcanet, 1982

Sylvia Townsend Warner, 'East Chaldon and T. F. Powys', *Powys Review* 7, 1980*

Sylvia Townsend Warner, *A Garland of Straw*, Chatto & Windus, 1943

Sylvia Townsend Warner, *Letters,* Chatto & Windus, 1982*

Sylvia Townsend Warner, *A Moral Ending*, William Jackson, 1931

Sylvia Townsend Warner, *The Salutation*, Chatto & Windus, 1932

Sylvia Townsend Warner, 'Theodore Powys and Some Friends at East Chaldon', *Powys Review* 5, 1979

Sylvia Townsend Warner, 'The Way by Which I Have Come', *The Countryman*, July 1939

Louis Wilkinson ('Louis Marlow'), *Swan's Milk*, Faber, 1934*

Louis Wilkinson, *Welsh Ambassadors*, Chapman & Hall, 1936*

II *Unpublished Sources*

Collection E. E. Bissell, (Powys Society) Documents concerning financial accounts of White House Farm, Sweffling, and the purchase of Beth Car; Theodore's account of himself, 1927; and the following letters:

       T. F. Powys to Sylvia Townsend Warner, 23.11.21, 19.3.23, 12.10.23, 18.7.24, .2. 8. 27

       Stephen Tomlin to T. F. Powys, undated (one postmarked 24.1.23)

       Sylvia Townsend Warner, to T. F. Powys, 7. 2. 25, 30.1 1?26, 8.4.30, 27.3.31

       Florence Hardy to Violet Powys, 8.11.25 [postmark]

Dorset County Museum, Letter Alyse Gregory to Sylvia Townsend Warner, n.d. [1967], 'Mrs Woodwright', typescript for broadcast by Elizabeth Muntz

Dorset Record Office, Sale catalogue of the Weld Estate, Chaldon portion, 1929

Dorset Record Office, Marriage Registers for Chaldon Herring, 1837 - 1964
Oliver Garnett, 'The Sculpture of Stephen Tomlin', unpublished dissertation
Garold Sharpe, Unpublished copy manuscript of T. F. Powys, *Cottage Shadows*
    Letter Sylvia Townsend Warner to Alyse Gregory, 20.6.67
University of Texas, Llewelyn Powys, Letter to Littleton Powys, 23.7.23
    T. F. Powys, *Amos Lear*, unpublished manuscript
    T. F. Powys, *Georgina, A Lady*, unpublished manuscript
    T. F. Powys, Letters to Ottoline Morrell, 1.10.24, 25.3.26
    T. F. Powys, Letters to J. C. Powys, 29.9.16, 2.7.17, 9.12.17, 4.1.18,
24.11.18, 8.11.20, 24.11.20?, 14.10.22, 12.12.24, 10.4.25
    T. F. Powys, Letter to Gertrude Powys, 7.3.41
    T. F. Powys, Letter to Katie Powys, 25.12.45
    Sylvia Townsend Warner, Letter to Frank Warren, 10.7.56
Personal information: Bea Howe, Francis Powys, Giles Wordsworth

3. *The Sailor's Return*
I *Published Sources*

Peter Clark, *The English Alehouse*, Longman, 1983
M. A. Crowther, *The Workhouse System*, 1834-1929, Methuen, 1983
Commission on the Employment of Children, Young Persons and Women in Agriculture, 1868-9 (XIII)
Dorset County Council, *Dorset Workhouses*, 1980
Mary Frampton, *Journal*, 1779 - 1846, Sampson Low, 1885
David Garnett (ed.), *Carrington*, Cape, 1970
David Garnett, *The Sailor's Return*, Chatto & Windus, 1925
Ronald Good, *The Old Roads of Dorset*, Bournemouth, 1966
Roger Guttridge, *Dorset Smugglers*, Dorset Pub. Co., 1984
Thomas Hardy, *Wessex Tales*, Macmillan, 1912
Pamela Horn, *The Rural World*, Hutchinson, 1980
E. J. Hobsbawm and George Rudé, *Captain Swing*, Lawrence & Wishart, 1969
Kelly's *Directory* for Dorsetshire, 1867-1939
Barbara Kerr, *Bound to the Soil*, John Baker, 1968
Luke Owen Pike, *A History of Crime in England* (Vol.II), Smith, Elder, 1876
John Cowper Powys, *Letters to his Brother Llewelyn* (Vol.I), Village Press, 1975
Llewelyn Powys, *Dorset Essays*, Redcliffe Press, 1983
Llewelyn Powys, 'The Sailor's Return', *New York Herald Tribune*, Dec. 6 1925
Llewelyn Powys, *Skin for Skin*, Cape, 1926
Jean Starr Untermeyer, *Private Collection*, Alfred A. Knopf, 1965
Sylvia Townsend Warner, 'East Chaldon and T. F. Powys', *Powys Review* 7, 1980
Sylvia Townsend Warner, *Letters*, Chatto & Windus, 1982
Sylvia Townsend Warner, 'Love Green', *The Nineteenth Century and After* (Vol. 112), August 1932

Sylvia Townsend Warner, 'Theodore Powys and Some Friends at East Chaldon', *Powys Review* 5, 1979

Sylvia Townsend Warner, 'The Way in Which I Have Come', *The Countryman* (XIX), 1939

Jimmy Young, *History of Better Pubs in Dorset*, Better Pubs, 1975

II *Unpublished Sources*

Collection E. E. Bissell (Powys Society), Letter Stephen Tomlin to Theodore Powys (undated), Letter Gerald Brenan to T.F.Powys n.d. [March 22 1932].

G. A. Body, 'Administration of the Poor Law in Dorset', unpublished thesis, 1967

Dorset County Library, Census returns for Chaldon Herring, 1851, 1861

Dorset County Museum, Diary of Sylvia Townsend Warner, Nov 13 1930

Dorset Record Office, Accounts of the Overseers of the Poor for Chaldon Herring, 1723-1836

Dorset Record Office, Papers relating to Edward Weld's Right of Wreck at Chaldon, 1768-9

Personal information: Ken and Josie Blandamer, Elizabeth Fishburn, Richard Garnett, Peter Powys Grey, Mrs Florence Legg, Mrs P. V. Marx, Rowland and Betty Miller, Mrs Frances Partridge, Francis Powys

4. *Church and School*

I *Published Sources*

Gerald Brenan, *Personal Record*, Cape, 1974

The Countryman, April-June, 1941.

Dorset County Chronicle, Feb. 6, 1902

Crockford's Clerical Directory, 1858-1978

David Garnett, *The Sailor's Return*, Chatto & Windus, 1925

Thomas Hardy, 'The Dorsetshire Labourer', *Thomas Hardy's Personal Writings* (ed. H. Orel), Macmillan, 1967

Claire Harman (ed.) 'Sylvia Townsend Warner 1893-1978: A Celebration', *PN Review* 23, 1981

Kenneth Hopkins, *The Powys Brothers*, Warren House, Norfolk, 1972

Pamela Horn, *The Victorian Country Child*, Roundwood Press, 1974

Kelly's *Directory* for Dorsetshire, 1867 - 1939

Theodore Francis Powys, *Come and Dine/Tadnol*, R. A. Brimmell, Hastings, 1967

Theodore Francis Powys, *Fables (No Painted Plumage)*, Chatto & Windus, 1929

Theodore Francis Powys, *The Only Penitent*, Chatto & Windus, 1931

Theodore Francis Powys, *The Two Thieves*, Chatto & Windus, 1932

Proceedings Dorset Natural History and Archaeological Society Nos. 13, 21 & 25

John S. Simon, *Methodism in Dorset*, Weymouth, 1870

Somerset and Dorset Notes and Queries Vol. XVIII, 1926

Sylvia Townsend Warner, *More Joy in Heaven*, Cresset Press, 1935

Sylvia Townsend Warner, *Whether a Dove or Seagull*, Chatto & Windus, 1934

See also items asterisked in ch. 2 above.

II *Unpublished Sources*
Collection E. E. Bissell (Powys Society), Letter T. F. Powys to Sylvia Townsend Warner 25.9.27, Theodore Powys's account of himself, 1927
Dorset County Library, Census for Chaldon Herring, 1861
Dorset County Museum, Diary of Sylvia Townsend Warner, Oct. 18 1953
Dorset Record Office, Chaldon Herring School Log, 1876-1918 (No. 17962)
Dorset Record Office, Churchwardens' Accounts for Chaldon Herring, 1708-1768, 1780-1880
Dorset Record Office, Record of Weymouth Methodist Circuit (additional)
Chaldon Trust Accounts 1905-1919
Guide to Chaldon Herring Parish Church, n.d. [1986?]
Rosemary Manning, Alyse Gregory's journal, 12.7.33
Rowland Miller
National Society for Promoting Religious Education, File on Chaldon Herring School, (EIO/52/20)
Univ. of Texas, papers concerning David Garnett and T.F. Powys's civil list pension
Letter Theodore Powys to John Cowper Powys, n.d.
Personal information: Jim Pitman, Garold Sharpe, Kenneth Skelton, John Vickers (World Methodist Historical Society)

5. *The Vicarage*
I *Published Sources*
Dorset County Chronicle, Jan. 24, 1935
Malcolm Elwin, *The Life of Llewelyn Powys*, Bodley Head, 1946
David Garnett, *The Familiar Faces*, Chatto & Windus, 1962
Richard Perceval Graves, *The Brothers Powys*, Routledge, 1983
Edna St. Vincent Millay, *Letters*, Harper & Bros., New York, 1952
The News of the World, Jan. 20/Jan. 27, 1935
The People, Jan. 20, 1935
John Cowper Powys, *Letters to his Brother Llewelyn* Vol.II, Village Press, 1975
Llewelyn Powys, *Letters,* Bodley Head, 1943
Llewelyn Powys, *The Twelve Months*, Bodley Head, 1936
T.F. Powys, *Innocent Birds*, Chatto & Windus, 1926
The Times, Jan. 21 & 22, 1935
Sylvia Townsend Warner, *Letters*, Chatto & Windus, 1982

II *Unpublished Sources*
Collection E. E. Bissell (Powys Society), 3 undated letters from Llewelyn Powys to Mr Dibben
Dorset County Museum, Letter Llewelyn Powys to Sylvia Townsend Warner, n.d.
Dorset Record Office, Chaldon Herring, Register of Services, 1915-1948
Rosemary Manning, Unpublished journal of Alyse Gregory

Letters Valentine Ackland to Alyse Gregory, July 29, n.d.
University of Texas, Papers concerning the Vicarage libel case, 1934-5
　　Diary of Gertrude Powys, 1935
　　Letter Llewelyn Powys to James Cobb, n.d. (from Clavadel)
　　Letter Llewelyn Powys to Gamel Woolsey, n.d. [1933]
　　Letters Theodore Powys to John Cowper Powys, n.d. [c. 1918], 24. 12.20
　　Letters Theodore Powys to Llewelyn Powys, 16.10.30, 26.12.30, 23.7.37
　　Letter Sylvia Townsend Warner to Violet Powys, 28.3.26
Personal information: Francis Powys

6. *Rat's Barn*
I *Published Sources*
Valentine Ackland, *Country Conditions*, Lawrence & Wishart, 1936
Valentine Ackland, *For Sylvia*, Chatto & Windus, 1985
Valentine Ackland, 'Grannie Moxon', *The Countryman*, Winter 1949
Valentine Ackland, *The Nature of the Moment*, Chatto & Windus, 1973
Valentine Ackland, 'The Village Witch', *West Country Magazine*, Autumn 1949
Valentine Ackland, *Whether a Dove or Seagull,* Chatto & Windus, 1934
Jennifer Clarke, *Exploring the West Country: A Woman's Guide*, Virago, 1987
Department of the Environment, *List of Buildings of Special Architectural or Historic Interest, District of Purbeck, Dorset,* 1984 (parishes of Affpuddle, Chaldon Herring etc.)
Richard Perceval Graves, *The Brothers Powys*, Routledge, 1983
Claire Harman (ed.), *Diaries of Sylvia Townsend Warner*, Chatto & Windus, 1994
Claire Harman, *Sylvia Townsend Warner,* Chatto & Windus, 1989
Holborn & West Central London Committee for Spanish Medical Aid, *Spain and Us*, n.d.
Belinda Humfrey (ed.), *Recollections of the Powys Brothers*, Peter Owen, 1980
Wendy Mulford, *This Narrow Place*, Pandora, 1988
Hope Muntz & Catherine Morton, *The Carmen de Hastingae Proelio*, O.U.P., 1972
Hope Muntz, *The Golden Warrior*, Chatto & Windus, 1948
Susanna Pinney (ed.), *I'll Stand By You, Letters of Sylvia Townsend Warner & Valentine Ackland*, Pimlico, 1998
Llewelyn Powys, *The Verdict of Bridlegoose*, Cape, 1927
Philippa Powys, *The Blackthorn Winter*, Constable, 1930
Philippa Powys, *Driftwood*, Blue Moon Booklets No. 6, E. Lahr, London, 1930
T. F. Powys, *Mockery Gap*, Chatto & Windus, 1925
Stephen Reynolds (with an introduction by Roy Hattersley), *A Poor Man's House*, O.U.P., 1982
Stephen Reynolds, *Seems So!*, Macmillan, 1911
Christopher Scoble, *Fisherman's Friend*, Halsgrove, 2000.
Brocard Sewell (ed.), *Theodore,* Saint Albert's Press, Aylesbury, 1964
Stone Industries, Review of Elizabeth Muntz's retrospective exhibition, Jan/ Feb. 1972

The Times, Obituary of Elizabeth Muntz, April 2, 1977
Sylvia Townsend Warner, *Collected Poems* (edited with an introduction by Claire Harman), Carcanet, 1982
Sylvia Townsend Warner, *Diaries* (ed. Harman), Chatto & Windus, 1994
Sylvia Townsend Warner, *Letters*, Chatto & Windus, 1982
Sylvia Townsend Warner, *Lolly Willowes*, Chatto & Windus, 1926
Sylvia Townsend Warner, *The Salutation*, Chatto & Windus, 1932

II *Unpublished Sources*
Gerard Casey, Journals of Katie Powys
Dorset County Museum, Papers concerning Sylvia Townsend Warner and Valentine Ackland. Unpublished poem to Granny Moxon by Sylvia Townsend Warner, letter Valentine Ackland to Hope Muntz, n.d..
Rosemary Manning, Unpublished letters from Valentine Ackland to Alyse Gregory, Jan 14, April 13, May 29, June 13, July 8?, Dec. 2, Dec. 9, 24.12.43, 13.3.44, 26.11.66, the remainder n.d.
Garold Sharpe, Unpublished letters from Alyse Gregory to Valentine Ackland, Dec. 18, 27.1.52? n.d.
University of Texas, Letter Valentine Ackland to Katie Powys, 22.8.26
    Alyse Gregory, 'Some Notes on C.E.P.P.' n.d [1963?]
    Papers on Catharine Edith Philippa (Katie) Powys, including *The Phoenix*, poems, stories, letters and journals
    Two letters of Katie Powys to Llewelyn Powys, c.1931
    Diaries of Gertrude Powys
    Letter T. F. Powys to Katie Powys, 16.2.40
    Letter T. F. Powys to Llewelyn Powys, 28.10.20
Personal information: Mrs Ros Benge-Abbott, Mrs Josie Blandamer, Louise de Bruin, Peter Powys Grey, Janet Machen, Mrs Hytie Mackintosh, Rowland Miller, Francis Powys.

7. *Chydyok*
I *Published Sources*
Gerald Brenan, *Personal Record*, Cape, 1974
Malcolm Elwin, *The Life of Llewelyn Powys*, Bodley Head, 1946
Richard Perceval Graves, *The Brothers Powys*, Routledge, 1983
Alyse Gregory, *The Cry of a Gull*, Ark Press, 1973
Alyse Gregory, *Hester Craddock*, Longman, 1931
Alyse Gregory, *King Log & Lady Lea*, Constable, 1929
Kenneth Hopkins, *Bertrand Russell and Gamel Woolsey*, Warren House,1985
Belinda Humfrey (ed.), Editorial to *Powys Review* 8, 1980/81
Edna St. Vincent Millay, *Huntsman, What Quarry?* Harper & Bros., 1939
Naomi Mitchison, *You May Well Ask*, Gollancz, 1979

Bibliography

Marianne Moore, *Selected Letters,* Faber, 1998
Post Office Circular, 1894
Llewelyn Powys, *A Baker's Dozen*, Bodley Head, 1941
Llewelyn Powys, *Book of Days*, Golden Cockerel Press, 1937
Llewelyn Powys, *Confessions of Two Brothers*, Sinclair Browne, 1982
Llewelyn Powys, *Dorset Essays,* Redcliffe Press, 1983
Llewelyn Powys, *Ebony and Ivory*, Grant Richards, 1923
Llewelyn Powys, *Glory of Life*, Bodley Head, 1934
Llewelyn Powys, *Impassioned Clay*, Longmans, 1931
Llewelyn Powys, *Letters* (with an introduction by Alyse Gregory), Bodley Head, 1943
Llewelyn Powys, *Love and Death*, Bodley Head, 1939
Llewelyn Powys, *Rats in the Sacristy*, Watts & Co., 1937
Llewelyn Powys, *Skin for Skin*, Cape, 1926
Llewelyn Powys, *Somerset and Dorset Essays*, Macdonald, 1957
Llewelyn Powys, *So Wild a Thing*, Ark Press, 1973
Llewelyn Powys, *The Twelve Months*, Bodley Head, 1936
Liewelyn Powys, *Thirteen Worthies*, Grant Richards, 1924
Llewelyn Powys, *The Verdict of Bridlegoose*, Cape, 1927
Gamel Woolsey, *Collected Poems*, Warren House, 1984
Gamel Woolsey, *Letters to Llewelyn Powys*, Warren House, 1983
Gamel Woolsey, *One Way of Love*, Virago, 1987

II *Unpublished Sources*
K. R. Bakes, recollections of East Chaldon postal services in the I920s and 1930s. Specially written for the present work, April 1987
Collection E. E. Bissell, (Powys Society) Letter Sylvia Townsend Warner to Theodore Powys, 20.12.26
Llewelyn Powys's specifications to his brother Albert Powys on improvements at Chydyok
Colegate University, Letters of Llewelyn Powys to Walter Miller, one dated Michaelmas Sunday, 1935
Dorset County Library, Census for Chaldon Herring, 1841, 1881
Rosemary Manning, Unpublished journals of Alyse Gregory, 1.10.24, 9.4.40. 30.5.40, 17.1.42, 12.4.43, 7.9.47, 28.9.47, 3.10.47, Tuesday December? 1947
Notice in the church of St. Catherine-by-the-sea, Holworth
Katie Powys, unpublished journals
Garold Sharpe, Letter Alyse Gregory to Valentine Ackland, 10.5.47
University of Texas, Uncollected writings of Llewelyn Powys, including 'A Downland Burden'.
Personal information: Ken Blandamer, Peter Powys Grey, Kenneth Hopkins, Janet Machen, Rowland and Betty Miller

Index